SOCIAL STUDIES

For the HiSET® Test

Photos courtesy of:
p. 8: © jsp; p. 8, p. 78: © Everett Historical; p. 9: © Cheryl Casey;
p. 13: © Maridav; p. 41: © Thomas Sztanek; p. 42: © chungking;
p. 142: © Election Assistance Commission; p. 148: © andrewgenn

Social Studies for the HiSET® Test
ISBN 978-1-56420-884-2

Copyright © 2016 New Readers Press
New Readers Press
ProLiteracy's Publishing Division
101 Wyoming Street, Syracuse, New York 13204
www.newreaderspress.com

All rights reserved. No part of this book may be reproduced or transmitted in any form or by any means, electronic or mechanical, including photocopying, recording, or by any information storage and retrieval system, without permission in writing from the publisher.

Printed in the United States of America
10 9 8 7

Proceeds from the sale of New Readers Press materials support professional development, training, and technical assistance programs of ProLiteracy that benefit local literacy programs in the U.S. and around the globe.

Developer: QuaraCORE
Editorial Director: Terrie Lipke
Cover Design: Carolyn Wallace
Technology Specialist: Maryellen Casey

HiSET® is a registered trademark of Educational Testing Service.
Trademarks are the property of their respective owners.

Contents

What to Expect 5
Pretest 6

Unit 1	**Geography**		**13**
	Lesson 1	Analyzing Maps	14
	Lesson 2	Geography Basics	18
	Lesson 3	Geographic Statistics and Models	24
	Lesson 4	Human Geography	30
	Unit Test		34
	Answer Key, Glossary, Study More!		**37**
Unit 2	**History**		**40**
	Lesson 1	World History: Pre-History and the Ancient World	41
	Lesson 2	World History: Classical Civilizations	43
	Lesson 3	Fact and Opinion	45
	Lesson 4	World History: The Early Modern Period	47
	Lesson 5	World History: A Globalized World	51
	Lesson 6	Reliability of Sources	55
	Lesson 7	U.S. History: Pre-Columbian Americas	57
	Lesson 8	U.S. History: Colonization and Settlement	61
	Lesson 9	U.S. History: The Early Republic	65
	Lesson 10	U.S. History: Civil War and Industrialization	69
	Lesson 11	U.S. History: The 20th Century	76
	Lesson 12	U.S. History: The Modern World	82
	Unit Test		86
	Answer Key, Glossary, Study More!		**91**
Unit 3	**Civics and Government**		**98**
	Lesson 1	Forms of Government	99
	Lesson 2	U.S. Founding Documents	101
	Lesson 3	Inferences and Conclusions	105
	Lesson 4	The U.S. Congress	107
	Lesson 5	The Changing Power of the President	111
	Lesson 6	Landmark Supreme Court Decisions	115
	Lesson 7	Elections	121
	Lesson 8	Special Interest Groups	125
	Lesson 9	Citizenship	127
	Lesson 10	State and Local Governments	131
	Lesson 11	Government Documents	135
	Unit Test		139
	Answer Key, Glossary, Study More!		**143**

Unit 4	Economics		148
	Lesson 1	Economic Basics	149
	Lesson 2	Economic Systems	153
	Lesson 3	Reading Charts, Graphs, and Tables	155
	Lesson 4	Economic Indicators	159
	Lesson 5	Government and the Economy	163
	Unit Test		167
	Answer Key, Glossary, Study More!		171

Practice Test and Practice Test Answer Key **174**

Using This Book

Welcome to *Social Studies for the HiSET® Test*, an important resource in helping you build a solid foundation of social studies skills as you prepare for the HiSET® high school equivalency test.

- First, read *What to Expect* on page 5, which will give you a brief overview of the HiSET® test itself.

- Next, take the Pretest, which begins on page 6. After taking the Pretest and checking your answers, use the chart on page 12 to find the lessons that will help you study the skills you need to improve.

- Then, start using the book, which is organized into four units, each containing brief lessons that focus on specific themes and skills. Important vocabulary terms included in the unit are listed on the first page of the unit and appear in **boldface** when they are first used in each lesson. Use the Glossary at the end of each unit to find key word definitions.

- Each lesson is followed by a Lesson Practice with questions to test your knowledge of the lesson content. Answers can be found in the Answer Key at the end of the unit. Each Lesson Practice also includes *Key Point!* and *Test Strategy* tips to help you prepare for the HiSET® test.

- Each unit concludes with a Unit Test that covers all the content in the unit's lessons. The Unit Test Answer Key appears at the end of each unit.

- Every unit concludes with *Study More!*, which lists additional skills and topics you can study to prepare for the HiSET® test.

- After completing all the units, you can test what you know by taking the HiSET® Practice Test, beginning on page 174. This test will help you check your understanding of all the skills in the book.

What to Expect

This book is intended to help you prepare to take the HiSET® (High School Equivalency Test) Exam in Social Studies. This is one of the five HiSET® exams; the others are in Mathematics, Reading, Writing, and Science. The HiSET® exams are available in English and in Spanish and can be taken in written format (on paper) or on a computer. For more information about the HiSET® exams, visit hiset.ets.org/test_takers.

Preparing for the Test

Using *Social Studies for the HiSET® Test* is a great first step in preparing to take the test. This book provides an overview of the content of the Social Studies test and gives you many opportunities to take practice tests to evaluate how well you know the content and skills that will be included in the HiSET® test.

Be sure to allow enough time to prepare for the test. Choose a test date that will not force you to rush through your study period. You need time to use this book, and possibly more time for additional review and practice tests.

When using this book, the Pretest helps you identify your strengths and weaknesses in social studies content and skills so you can pinpoint the areas on which to focus your study for the HiSET®.

Taking the Social Studies Test

The HiSET® Social Studies exam includes 50 multiple-choice questions. You will have 70 minutes to complete the test.

The Social Studies exam will assess your understanding of key content and skills taught in high school, including:

- United States history
- world history
- civics and citizenship
- government
- economics
- geography

These and many other topics are reviewed in this book. Each lesson covers a specific topic, and each is followed by practice questions to help you learn the content. Some lessons in this book show you how to read and interpret key documents, maps, and other images, which are skills you will need to use when you take the HiSET® Social Studies test.

After you complete the practice HiSET® test at the end of this book, you can judge your results and decide if you are ready to take the HiSET® Social Studies test.

PRETEST — Social Studies

Answer the following questions to gauge your readiness to take the HiSET® test. Answers to questions can be found on page 11.

Questions 1–3 refer to the following map.

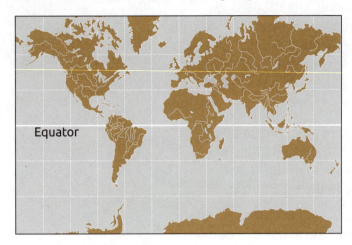

1. Which of the following BEST describes the image shown here?
   A a thematic representation
   B a Mercator map
   C a projection map
   D a latitude and longitude chart

2. Which is the most accurate statement about the Equator?
   A divides the Eastern and Western hemispheres
   B passes through Greenwich in the United Kingdom
   C divides the Northern and Southern hemispheres
   D passes through North America

3. Which of the following regions is MOST accurately represented here?
   A the Tropics
   B the Polar Regions
   C the Western Hemisphere
   D the Northern Hemisphere

4. What kind of an economy is one without money MOST likely to be?
   A command
   B market
   C mixed
   D traditional

5. Which of the following is MOST directly associated with the birth of democracy?
   A Rome
   B China
   C Sparta
   D Athens

6. Historians call the period following the fall of the Roman Empire
   A the Dark Ages.
   B the Renaissance.
   C the Reformation.
   D the Hagia Sophia.

7. Which of the following phrases would MOST likely appear in a description of population density?
   A at birth
   B per square mile
   C degrees latitude
   D per 1,000 people

8. Who is credited with establishing the Eastern Roman Empire during the 300s?
   A   Nero
   B   Justinian
   C   Augustus
   D   Constantine

9. Which of the following is a demographic indicator?
   A   elevation
   B   birth rate
   C   temperature
   D   physical geography

10. Which of the following MOST accurately describes the economy of the United States?
    A   It is a mixed economy.
    B   It is a pure market economy.
    C   It is a traditional economy.
    D   It is a command economy.

Questions 11 and 12 refer to the following image.

11. The form in the image is an example of a _____.
    A   CDL
    B   naturalization document
    C   functional document
    D   proclamation

12. Which of the following MOST closely falls into the same category as this form?
    A   a social security card
    B   a vehicle title
    C   a high school diploma
    D   a job application

13. Beginning in the 1400s, the Middle Passage was a trade route that ran from
    A   Africa to Europe.
    B   Europe to Africa.
    C   Africa to the Americas.
    D   North America to Africa.

Questions 14 and 15 refer to the following image.

Ancient Egyptian mural of grain harvest

14. The activity in the picture above is believed by historians to have permitted early humans to
    A develop spoken language.
    B hunt animals.
    C form permanent settlements.
    D live in mobile groups.

15. The food surpluses created by this activity allowed some early humans to engage in other pursuits. This development is called
    A agriculture.
    B cuneiform interpretation.
    C labor specialization.
    D polytheism.

16. Most of the problems that sparked World War I arose from widespread
    A militarism and nationalism.
    B militarism and isolationism.
    C progressivism and militarism.
    D progressivism and isolationism.

17. Nations in which region were MOST directly affected by the fall of the Soviet Union?
    A Central Asia
    B Eastern Europe
    C the Middle East
    D Western Europe

18. Every state legislature except that of Nebraska is modeled after
    A the United States Congress.
    B the council-management system.
    C the mayor-council system.
    D the state's executive branch.

Questions 19 and 20 refer to the following image.

19. Which of the following names the type of government headed by an authority such as the one shown in the image?
    A a monarchy
    B a democracy
    C a dictatorship
    D a theocracy

20. Which of the following terms BEST helps describe that government when its authority is shared with elected representatives?
    A communist
    B parliamentary
    C absolute
    D military

21. Which of the following means the same thing as *meridian*?
    A Equator
    B latitude line
    C hemisphere
    D longitude line

22. A nation whose government makes its economic decisions is said to have a
    A market economy.
    B command economy.
    C traditional economy.
    D mixed economy.

23. The central issue of economics is defined as the problem of _____.
    A surplus
    B scarcity
    C demand
    D capital

Questions 24 and 25 refer to the following image.

24. Acceptance of the text shown here led to the adoption of
    A the Articles of Confederation.
    B the Declaration of Independence.
    C the Treaty of Paris.
    D the United States Constitution.

25. The document adopted after this text was added replaced
    A the Articles of Confederation.
    B the United States Constitution.
    C the Declaration of Independence.
    D the Federalist Papers.

26. Which of the following is an accurate statement about the legislative branch of the federal government?
    A Each state has equal authority in the Senate but not in the House of Representatives.
    B Each state has equal authority in the House of Representatives but not in the Senate.
    C A Supreme Court ruling is considered the final word on a law's constitutionality.
    D A Supreme Court ruling is subject to approval or rejection by both houses of Congress.

27. Which of the following was a precedent set by President George Washington?
    A the administration of checks and balances
    B the practice of court packing
    C the establishment of a presidential Cabinet
    D the creation of an executive branch of government

Question 28 refers to the following passage.

> "It is emphatically the province and duty of the judicial department to say what the law is.
>
> Those who apply the rule to particular cases must of necessity expound and interpret that rule. If two laws conflict with each other, the courts must decide on the operation of each."
>
> — Chief Justice John Marshall, *Marbury* v. *Madison* (1803)

28. Which of the following names the check on legislative power being affirmed here?
    A presidential veto
    B executive privilege
    C judicial activism
    D judicial review

29. Which of the following did George Washington see as a threat to liberty?
    A political parties
    B political action committees
    C general elections
    D lobbyists

30. Which type of economy is the LEAST influenced by governmental decisions?
    A traditional
    B mixed
    C market
    D command

Questions 31–35 refer to the following graph.

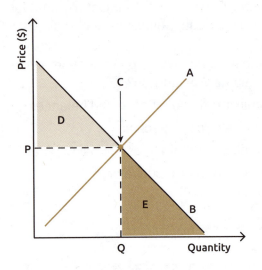

Complete each sentence with one of the terms listed below. Each term is used exactly one time.

| demand   equilibrium   shortage |
| supply   surplus |

31. Line A on the graph indicates how much of a good or a service producers are making. It is the _____ line.

32. Line B indicates how much of a good or a service consumers are willing to buy. It is the _____ line.

33. Point C on the graph indicates the point at which producers are providing exactly as much of a good or service as consumers will buy. It is the point of market _____.

34. Region D on the graph indicates when consumers want more of a good or service than producers are making. Activity in that region indicates a _____.

35. Region E on the graph indicates when consumers want less of a good or service than producers are making. Activity in that region indicates a _____.

Complete each sentence with one of the terms listed below. Each term is used exactly one time.

| Afghanistan   citizens   hemispheres |
| Iraq   lobbyists |

36. The United States attacked _____ in response to that nation's support of those who attacked the World Trade Center in 2001.

37. _____ work closely with government leaders on behalf of special interest groups.

38. Immigrants who wish to become U.S. _____ are required to go through a process called naturalization.

39. Both the Equator and the prime meridian divide our world into _____.

40. Both the 1990s Persian Gulf War and the 2000s War on Terror involved armed conflict between the United States and _____.

Answer Key — PRETEST

1. B.
2. C.
3. A.
4. D.
5. D.
6. A.
7. B.
8. D.
9. B.
10. A.
11. C.
12. D.
13. C.
14. C.
15. C.
16. A.
17. B.
18. A.
19. A.
20. B.
21. D.
22. B.
23. B.
24. D.
25. A.
26. A.
27. C.
28. D.
29. A.
30. C.
31. supply
32. demand
33. equilibrium
34. shortage
35. surplus
36. Afghanistan
37. lobbyists
38. citizens
39. hemispheres
40. Iraq

PRETEST Answer Key

Check your answers. Review the questions you did not answer correctly. You can use the chart below to locate lessons in this book that will help you learn more about social studies content and skills. Which lessons do you need to study? Work through the book, paying close attention to the lessons in which you missed the most questions. At the end of the book, you will have a chance to take another test to see how much your score improves.

Question	Where to Look for Help		
	Unit	Lesson	Pages
1, 3	1	1	14
2, 7, 21, 39	1	2	18–20
4, 10, 22, 30	4	2	153
5	2	2	43
6, 8	2	4	47
9	1	3	24
11, 12	3	11	135
13	2	5	52
14, 15	2	1	41
16, 17	2	11	76–77
18	3	10	131
19	3	5	112
20	3	1	99
23, 31, 32, 33, 34, 35	4	1	149–150
24, 25	3	2	101
26	3	4	107
27	3	5	111
28	3	6	115
29	3	7	121
36, 40	2	12	82
37	3	8	125
38	3	9	127

UNIT 1

Geography

The HiSET® Social Studies test covers several content areas. One of these is geography. Geography questions will include concepts and key terms related to both physical and human geography. To answer HiSET® geography questions, you may have to analyze maps, graphs, diagrams, or datasets. You will be asked to look at economic, political, and social factors related to real and fictitious case studies. In this unit, you will review the basics of geography. You will learn how to identify and analyze maps. You will also learn how to work with data and use geographic models.

KEY WORDS

- birth rate
- climate
- climate change
- climate map
- compass rose
- concentric zone model
- cultural diffusion
- death rate
- demographic
- demographic transition mode
- economic map
- Equator
- hemisphere
- human geography
- infant mortality rate
- key
- latitude
- legend
- life expectancy
- longitude
- map projection
- Mercator projection
- migration
- physical geography
- physical map
- political map
- population density
- population pyramid
- prime meridian
- scale
- thematic map
- weather

UNIT 1 / LESSON 1

Analyzing Maps

KEY WORDS

- climate map
- compass rose
- economic map
- key
- legend
- map projection
- Mercator projection
- physical map
- political map
- scale
- thematic map

Map Features

Geographic information on the HiSET® often appears on a map. Learning to read and analyze maps is therefore important to success on these types of questions. Maps show many different kinds of information, but they share features in common. Maps usually have titles that give information about their contents. A title might tell the region, topic, or year that the map represents. Maps that use symbols to show details typically have a map **key**. The key shows each symbol and its meaning. For example, a key might tell the map user that a star stands for a national capital. Map keys are also called **legends**. Maps also have a **scale** to indicate how that map presents distance, and a **compass rose** to show north, south, east, and west.

Follow the steps below to use a map's features to answer questions.

> **Step 1**: Read the map's title. What main information does the map show?

> **Step 2**: Determine what places are shown on the map. Does it show the world, a specific continent, a country, or a smaller region?

> **Step 3**: Study the map's legend. Identify any special symbols or shading used on the map.

> **Step 4**: Read the questions associated with the map. Figure out which information from the map is needed to help you answer the question correctly. Use the map's features to locate and interpret this information.

Maps that show the same information might look different due to the mapmaker's choice of **map projection**. A map projection is the way in which the round Earth is transferred to a flat map. Maps are never completely accurate because of this flattening of Earth's features. The **Mercator projection**, developed in the 1500s, is one common map projection. The Mercator projection distorts, or changes, the scale of places that are farther from the Equator. As a result, places in the far north and far south look larger than they actually are.

Analyzing Maps

Types of Maps

Geographers use many different types of maps to organize information. Some common map types appear below.

Map	Definition	
Climate map	Shows information about the usual weather in a place	**Contiguous U.S. Climate Zones** — COOL, TEMPERATE, HOT-HUMID, HOT-ARID. Source: U.S. Dept. of Energy
Physical map	Shows information about landforms and bodies of water	**Contiguous United States** — Feet/Meters: 10000/3050, 5000/1525, 2000/610, 1000/305, 500/153. Pacific Coast, Sierra Nevada and Cascade Mts., Great Basin, Rocky Mountains, Great Plains, Appalachian Mts., Atlantic Coastal Plain
Political map	Shows borders and capital cities	**United States** — CAPITAL CITIES

Lesson 1 / Analyzing Maps

Analyzing Maps

Map	Definition	
Economic map	Shows economic information like the locations of resources	**Oil and Coal Resource in the Contiguous United States** Coal / Oil Source: Office of U.S. Rep. Bob Latta
Thematic map	Shows information about a particular subject, like voting patterns, sites of military conflicts, or population patterns	**U.S. Presidential Election Results, 2012** Obama (D) / Romney (R)

Lesson Practice

UNIT 1 / LESSON 1

Complete the activities below to check your understanding of the lesson content.

Apply Your Knowledge

Label each feature of the map shown below.

California's Major Cities ①

1. _____
2. _____
3. _____
4. _____

Skills Practice

5. Dr. Jefferson is conducting a study of the best places in the United States to open a solar energy collection plant. What kind of map would be most helpful for her study?

    A thematic map of kinds of power people use
    B physical map of rivers and major landforms
    C economic map of domestic coal reserves
    D climate map focusing on sunny and cloudy days

6. A road map could best be considered a special type of which of the following maps?

    A physical map   C thematic map
    B climate map   D political map

See page 37 for answers and help.

Lesson 1 / Analyzing Maps

KEY POINT!

The different parts of a map contain different kinds of information. Often, you need to connect this information to draw conclusions.

TEST STRATEGY

Remember to read all the answer choices before making your selection to ensure that you do not miss the correct answer. Read Question 5. This question asks you to conclude what kind of map best tells about the distribution of a resource needed to produce solar energy. First, you must determine what kind of resource is needed: sunlight. Then, read each answer choice to find the map that will best show where sunlight is found. You might be tempted by choices that tell about other forms of power or other kinds of physical features. All of these maps may be of some help to Dr. Jefferson. By reading each choice, however, you can determine that D is the best choice for her study.

17

UNIT 1 / LESSON 2: Geography Basics

KEY WORDS

- climate
- Equator
- hemisphere
- latitude
- longitude
- physical geography
- population density
- prime meridian
- weather

Physical Geography

Many geography questions require understanding and applying information about **physical geography**. Physical geography relates to Earth's physical features. These include landforms, bodies of water, terrain, and **climate**. Some questions might ask just for the identification of these features. Others demand interpretation or critical thinking. They might relate to comparing patterns, drawing inferences and conclusions, or making predictions.

The HiSET® also tests how physical geography affects human activity on Earth's surface. A set of geography questions will likely include at least one that connects physical features to human factors like population, transportation, or culture. For example, people tend to settle near places with certain physical characteristics; cities are often located on waterways or near good agricultural land. Looking for these connections will help you do your best on the test.

Organizing Earth's Surface

Geographers organize Earth according to its physical geography. They also organize its surface using a system of imaginary lines known as **latitude** and **longitude**. Latitude lines circle the Earth from east to west. Longitude lines, also known as meridians, circle Earth from north to south. Because Earth is a sphere, latitude and longitude lines are measured in degrees. The **Equator** is the central line of latitude, so it is labeled 0°. The Equator passes through the hottest parts of Earth, like Central America and northern Africa. The **prime meridian** is the central line of longitude. It passes through Greenwich, near London, in the United Kingdom. Scientists chose this meridian as the central one without any special geographic reason.

The Equator and the prime meridian divide Earth into **hemispheres**. A hemisphere is one-half of Earth. The Northern and Southern Hemispheres are north and south of the Equator. The Western and Eastern Hemispheres lie to the west and east of the prime meridian.

Geography Basics

UNIT 1 / LESSON 2

Applying Physical Geography

Physical features often influence where people settle. They also influence the **population density** of a place. Population density is a measure of how many people live within a set land area, like a square mile or square kilometer. Places with low-lying, flat terrain are easier to build on, so most major cities are located on this kind of physical geography. Other places have physical features that are more challenging. Mountains, thick forests, deserts, and swamps discourage dense settlement.

China's Physical and Population Geography

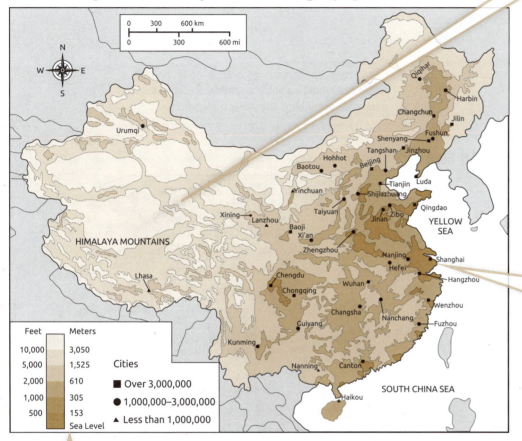

This region has very high elevations. It also has few cities. This pattern suggests a mountainous, rural area with a low population density. Why might mountainous regions be difficult to settle?

Shanghai and other very large cities are located in areas with low elevations. They are also located near waterways or coastal areas. These provide not only water but also access to trade and transportation routes. These cities have probably grown due to the favorability of their physical geography.

Notice that some places have low elevations and are relatively flat. Others have very high elevations and are probably mountains. The map also identifies major cities and gives their population ranges.

Geography Basics

Applying Latitude and Longitude

Geography questions often focus on the relationships among physical systems and processes. For example, the test might address systems like **weather** and climate. Weather is a measure of the atmospheric conditions, such as temperature, wind, and precipitation, in a place at a certain time. Climate is the usual weather in a place over time.

A place's location has a great effect on what its climate is like. Places near the Equator receive more direct light and energy from the sun. They have some of the hottest climates on Earth. Landforms like mountains and bodies of water also contribute to climatic patterns.

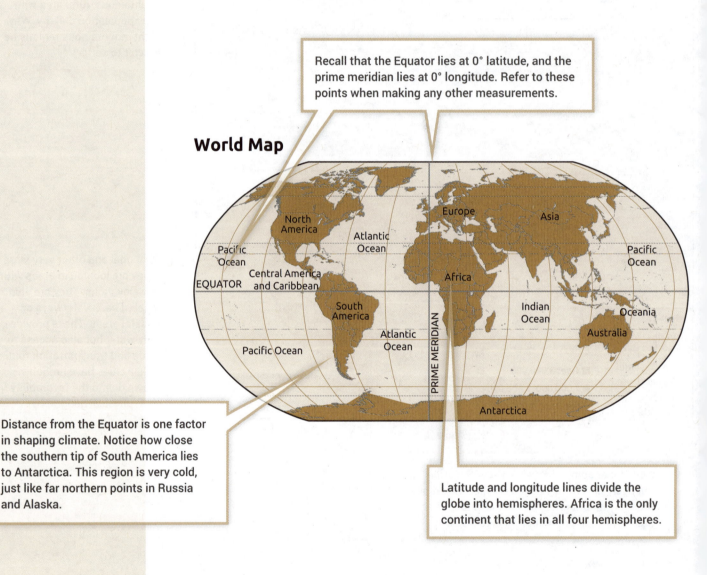

Recall that the Equator lies at 0° latitude, and the prime meridian lies at 0° longitude. Refer to these points when making any other measurements.

Distance from the Equator is one factor in shaping climate. Notice how close the southern tip of South America lies to Antarctica. This region is very cold, just like far northern points in Russia and Alaska.

Latitude and longitude lines divide the globe into hemispheres. Africa is the only continent that lies in all four hemispheres.

Lesson Practice

UNIT 1 / LESSON 2

Complete the activities below to check your understanding of the lesson content.

Vocabulary

Write definitions in your own words for each of the key terms.

1. climate _____
   _____

2. hemisphere _____
   _____

3. population density _____
   _____

4. prime meridian _____
   _____

UNIT 1 / LESSON 2

Lesson Practice

KEY POINT!

Geographers use lines of latitude and longitude to organize Earth into hemispheres. Latitude and longitude can be used to find any location on a map.

Skills Practice

Questions 5-8 refer to the map.

Australia

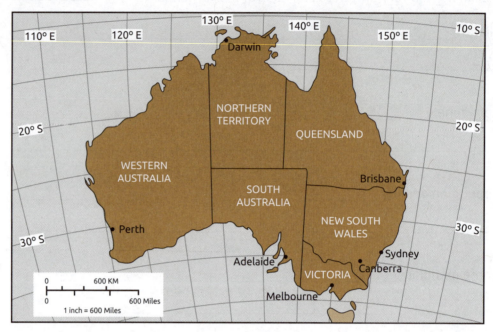

5. An airplane is flying directly from Sydney to Brisbane. About how many miles will it fly?

   A   200 miles

   B   450 miles

   C   750 miles

   D   1000 miles

Unit 1 / Geography

Lesson Practice

UNIT 1 / LESSON 2

6. Which longitude line runs closest to Adelaide?
   A 20°S
   B 40°S
   C 120°E
   D 140°E

7. Which conclusion can be drawn about Australia based on this map?
   A Areas along Australia's coasts are likely low-lying and flat.
   B Climatic conditions are similar across Australia.
   C Australia's population is likely the densest near its center.
   D Australia is the smallest continental landform on Earth.

8. Silvie lives in a place located at 30°S latitude and 130°E longitude. Which Australian state does she live in?
   A Tasmania
   B South Australia
   C New South Wales
   D Northern Territory

See page 37 for answers and help.

TEST STRATEGY

Sometimes, a question might give you details that you do not need in order to find the right answer. You might find it helpful to rewrite the question in order to answer it more easily. To do this, restate the question in your own words. Read Question 8. This question could be restated as, In what Australian state is 30°S latitude and 130°E longitude located? Find the answer by putting your finger on the intersection of these two lines on the map.

UNIT 1 / LESSON 3: Geographic Statistics and Models

KEY WORDS

- birth rate
- concentric zone model
- death rate
- demographic
- demographic transition model
- infant mortality rate
- life expectancy
- population pyramid

Population Statistics

Geographers study the physical world. They also study the way of life of people in different places. The study of populations is called demographics. The HiSET® might require interpretation and analysis of **demographic** statistics as part of the Social Studies test. Understanding different types of demographic indicators allows people to draw conclusions about what life is like in a given place.

Common demographic indicators measure facts and figures about a population. The **birth rate** tells the number of babies born each year per 1,000 people. The **death rate** tells how many people out of 1,000 die each year. The **infant mortality** rate tells how many babies under one year of age die out of 1,000. These rates help geographers to draw conclusions about how quickly a population is likely to grow or shrink. They also suggest information about family sizes, health care, and the role of women. Places with low birth rates and low infant mortality rates, for example, tend to be highly developed. Women and children have good nutrition and good health care.

Geographic Models

Geographic information is often shown on maps. However, some types of geographic information can be presented in other ways. Tables, graphs, and charts can give demographic statistics. A **population pyramid** shows the distribution of a population by gender and age. Certain geographic ideas are usually presented using models. Models can visually show abstract ideas.

Two important geographic models are the **demographic transition model** and the **concentric zone model**. These show different ideas about populations. The demographic transition model offers a way to explain changing stages of population growth. To do this, it applies the birth rate and death rate. The concentric zone model attempts to explain the physical growth of cities. It suggests that cities have a dense urban business center surrounded by rings of homes, businesses, and industries.

Geographic Statistics and Models

UNIT 1 / LESSON 3

Interpreting Demographic Data

Geography questions might require the interpretation of a map or other source giving demographic information. Use the map title and legend to determine what the source shows, and look for any overall patterns that could give evidence for inferences or conclusions. Some questions might ask you simply to find and restate data. Others will ask you to make connections between that data and the likely conditions in a place.

Life expectancy, or the number of years the average person lives, is one common type of demographic indicator. Think of all of the factors that contribute to how long a person lives. Nutrition, access to clean water and sanitation, and availability of health care all make a difference. Problems like civil war can also lower life expectancies.

The title tells you what data this map shows—life expectancy as measured for people born in 2003. Life expectancy can vary over time due to changes in a population's overall health.

Life Expectancy at Birth, 2003

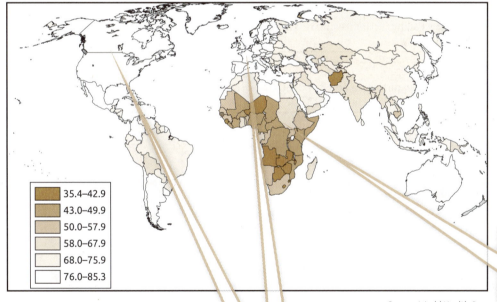

Source: World Health Org.

Legend:
- 35.4–42.9
- 43.0–49.9
- 50.0–57.9
- 58.0–67.9
- 68.0–75.9
- 76.0–85.3

North America and Western Europe have high life expectancies. These places benefit from access to a wide variety of food, advanced health care, and stable governments that provide services like water and trash disposal.

Some of the lowest life expectancies are in sub-Saharan Africa. Low economic development, high rates of infectious disease, and poor access to health care all contribute to these levels.

UNIT 1 / LESSON 3

Geographic Statistics and Models

Applying Geographic Models

Geography questions often focus on the relationships among physical systems and processes. For example, the test might address systems like weather and climate. Weather is a measure of the atmospheric conditions, such as temperature, wind, and precipitation, in a place at a certain time. Climate is the usual weather in a place over time.

A place's location has a great effect on what its climate is like. Places near the Equator receive more direct light and energy from the sun. They have some of the hottest climates on Earth. Landforms like mountains and bodies of water also contribute to climatic patterns.

Demographic Transition Model

Stage One
- High birth rate and high death rate; stable population

> Populations cannot grow much during this stage despite the high birth rate. Many young people die from untreated diseases like influenza or tuberculosis. Women might die in childbirth.

Stage Two
- High birth rate and declining death rate; rapidly growing population

Stage Three
- Falling birth rate and relatively low death rate; slowly growing population

> These stages result as countries have better methods of production. More food and better health care help people live longer. As children survive to adulthood, women tend to have fewer babies and are more likely to be educated.

Stage Four
- Low birth rate and low death rate; stable population

> This stage describes highly developed industrial countries like the United States. Can you think of another example of a country likely to be in this development stage?

Lesson Practice — UNIT 1 / LESSON 3

Complete the activities below to check your understanding of the lesson content.

Check Your Understanding

Write complete sentences to answer each of the following questions.

1. What are two examples of demographic statistics studied by geographers?

   _____

   _____

   _____

2. What is an advantage of using a geographic model?

   _____

   _____

3. Dr. Lopez is studying the development of two cities. One is Newcastle, England, which developed as an industrial center during the 1700s and 1800s. The other is Shenzen, China, which has experienced rapid industrial growth in the 2000s. Which geographic model should Dr. Lopez use to compare these cities, and why?

   _____

   _____

   _____

   _____

   _____

Lesson 3 / Geographic Statistics and Models

UNIT 1 / LESSON 3

Lesson Practice

KEY POINT!

Analyzing demographic statistics on maps allows you to compare and contrast patterns across places and regions.

Skills Practice

Study the map. Then choose the correct answer to each question.

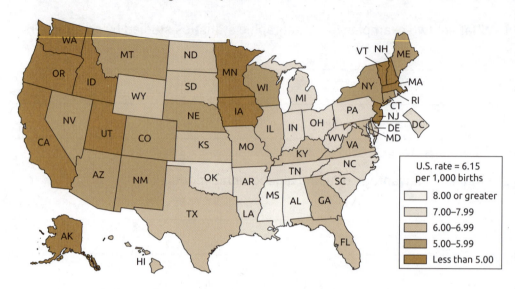

U.S. Infant Mortality Rate, 2010

4. A geographer would most likely use this map to study which of the following?

   A U.S. population growth by state

   B economic activities in different U.S. states

   C access to women's health services across the United States

   D internal migration patterns within the United States

Lesson Practice

UNIT 1 / LESSON 3

5. Which conclusion does this map best support?
   - A Child care and nutrition vary across the United States.
   - B Children born in the West are comparatively disadvantaged.
   - C People living in the Southeast are more likely to live in rural areas.
   - D Fewer hospitals exist in the Midwest than in other parts of the country.

6. In which of the following states is a newborn infant most likely to die before reaching age one?
   - A Alabama
   - B Georgia
   - C Oklahoma
   - D Washington

7. Based on the map, which state has the highest birth rate?
   - A Alaska
   - B Louisiana
   - C New York
   - D There is not enough information to make this determination.

See page 37 for answers and help.

TEST STRATEGY

Do you often struggle to choose between two answers? Try covering the answer choices with your hand as you read the question. Then, find your own answer to the question before reviewing the answer choices. Try this with Question 6. This question asks for a straightforward piece of information—the state with the highest infant mortality rates. Study the map. The two states with the highest rates are Alabama and Louisiana. Now, review the answer choices. The answer must be A.

UNIT 1 / LESSON 4 — Human Geography

KEY WORDS

- climate change
- cultural diffusion
- human geography
- migration

Fields of Human Geography

When you think of geography, you probably think of landforms, climate, and other physical features. Geography as a whole also includes the study of **human geography**. Human geography is the study of how people interact with not only the land but also with broad regional systems. The HiSET® might require an understanding of human geography. It might also ask you to connect physical features to human systems in order to perform analysis.

The study of populations is one part of human geography. Human geographers look at more than just statistics, however. They investigate **migration**, which is the movement of people. They also consider how ideas and practices spread from place to place. This process is known as **cultural diffusion**. Often, these processes are interrelated. People who settle in a new place bring along ideas and practices from their previous home.

Human geography considers the nature and role of those ideas in building societies. Human geographers study religious practices in different groups, for example. They investigate how people build and maintain systems of government. They also study how people make a living and organize trade.

Finally, human geography investigates how humans use and change the land and environment. Food production and the spread of crops are part of this system. So are issues relating to **climate change**, or the global shift in temperatures and climate patterns over time.

Human Geography
UNIT 1 / LESSON 4

Analyzing Cultural Diffusion

The spread of Bantu languages is one common example of cultural diffusion. Bantu people spread across all of sub-Saharan Africa thousands of years ago. They carried agricultural techniques, iron technology, and their languages with them. Today, millions of people in sub-Saharan Africa speak related languages. These are part of the Bantu family.

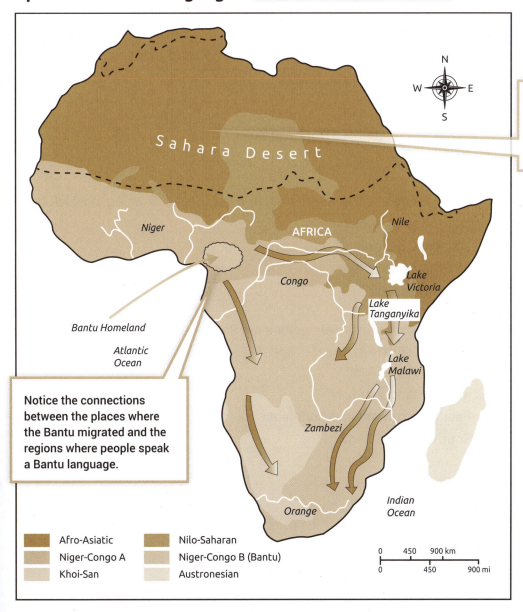

Spread of Bantu Languages

This map gives two main pieces of information. It tells where Bantu people spread and what languages are spoken in different regions of Africa today.

The Bantu did not spread north to this region. Why not? A large physical barrier—the Sahara Desert—blocked their path.

Notice the connections between the places where the Bantu migrated and the regions where people speak a Bantu language.

Legend:
- Afro-Asiatic
- Niger-Congo A
- Khoi-San
- Nilo-Saharan
- Niger-Congo B (Bantu)
- Austronesian

UNIT 1 / LESSON 4

Lesson Practice

Complete the activities below to check your understanding of the lesson content.

Skills Practice

Study the map. Then choose the correct answer to each question.

Election of 2012

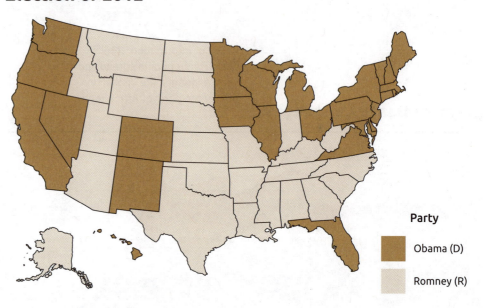

1. This map would be most interesting to a geographer working in which field?
   A cultural geography
   B economic geography
   C physical geography
   D political geography

2. Based on this map, in which regions did Barack Obama have the strongest support from voters?
   A Northeast and West
   B Midwest and South
   C Pacific Northwest and Southeast
   D Southwest and Midwest

TEST STRATEGY

The process of elimination is an effective way to find the best answer. Try this strategy on Question 1. Read the question. Then review the map. Now, read the first answer. Ask yourself, Does this map relate to cultural geography? It does not, so read the second choice. Repeat the process. Continue until you reach the correct answer, political geography.

Lesson Practice

UNIT 1 / LESSON 4

3. Based on this map, which conclusion about the 2012 presidential election is best supported?
   A   Mitt Romney won the popular vote but not the electoral vote.
   B   Voters within a region tend to hold similar opinions.
   C   The election was inconclusive.
   D   Barack Obama was supported by all of the same states as in 2008.

4. Which of the following tools would best help a geographer analyze trends in U.S. support for a president's policies?
   A   maps from the 2000, 2004, and 2008 presidential elections
   B   newspaper articles written in support of a particular candidate
   C   speeches given by President Obama in the 2012 presidential campaign
   D   a table showing the political affiliations of members of the House of Representatives

See page 37 for answers and help.

KEY POINT!

Human geographers study many categories of human life. Human geography includes economics, culture, social patterns, government, and land use.

UNIT 1 — Unit Test

Answer the questions based on the content covered in this unit.

1. Which of the following describes a problem with the Mercator map projection?
   A It cannot be organized using latitude and longitude lines.
   B It misrepresents the relative sizes of landforms and oceans.
   C It does not show all the places known to exist on Earth.
   D It can show only physical but not human features.

2. Lara is a travel agent. She is planning a trip for a client who wishes to visit as many state and provincial capitals as possible. Which type of map should she use to help her plan this trip?
   A climate map of North America
   B physical map of Mexico and Central America
   C political map of the United States and Canada
   D economic map of the Midwest and Northeast

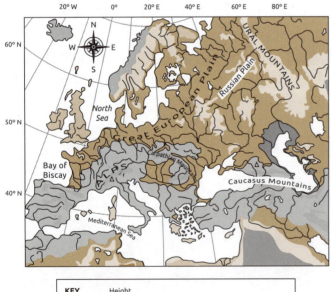

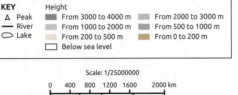

Questions 3–6 refer to the map below.

3. What is the best title for this map?
   A Members of the European Union
   B Sites of World War I and World War II
   C Routes Across the Atlantic Ocean
   D Physical Features of Europe

4. Which region likely has the densest population?
   A Alps
   B Great European Plain
   C Iberian Peninsula
   D Mediterranean Sea

5. A scientist releases a weather balloon near the intersection of the prime meridian and 60° north latitude. What is the closest physical feature to this site?
   A Russian Plain
   B Bay of Biscay
   C Apennine Mountains
   D North Sea

6. An airplane travels from the Mediterranean Sea across the Alps to the Scandinavian region. In which direction is it mostly going?
   A north
   B northwest
   C east
   D southeast

Questions 7–10 refer to the information in the table.

Country	Population size (in millions)	Population Growth Rate (in %)	Birth Rate	Death rate	Infant Mortality Rate	Life Expectancy (in years)
Bangladesh	169.0	1.6	21.14	5.61	44.09	70.9
El Salvador	6.1	0.25	16.46	5.69	17.86	74.4
Japan	126.9	−0.16	7.93	9.51	2.08	84.5
Sudan	36.1	1.72	29.19	7.66	51.52	63.4
United States	321.4	0.78	12.49	8.15	5.87	79.7

Source: CIA World Factbook

7. Based on this table, which prediction about Japan's population is best supported?
   A It will reach 130 million within ten years.
   B It will grow sharply as infant mortality declines.
   C Its median age will increase over time.
   D Its gender composition will become increasingly male.

8. Which of these countries most likely has the most barriers to access to health care for women and children?
   A Bangladesh
   B El Salvador
   C Sudan
   D United States

9. In which stage of the demographic transition model is Sudan best categorized?
   A Stage 1
   B Stage 2
   C Stage 3
   D Stage 4

10. Which country shown on this table has the lowest death rate?
    A Bangladesh
    B Japan
    C Sudan
    D United States

UNIT 1 — Unit Test

Questions 11–13 refer to the map below.

OPEC (Organization of the Petroleum Exporting Countries) is an association of countries engaged in the production and sale of oil. The members of OPEC collaborate to set production targets in order to influence global prices for oil.

OPEC Member Nations

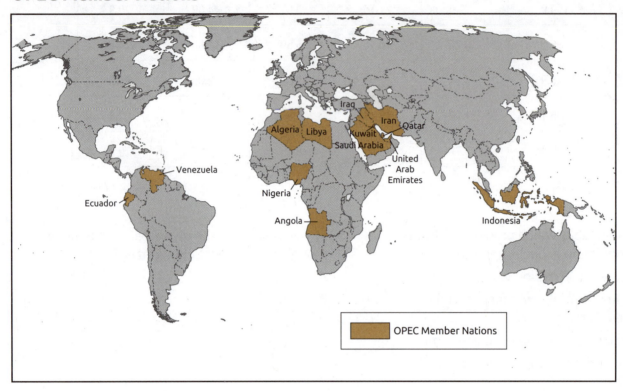

11. Based on this map, which region of the world has the richest oil reserves?
    - A Central and South America
    - B Sub-Saharan Africa
    - C Southwest Asia
    - D Northern and Western Europe

12. Which inference is best supported by this map?
    - A Countries with oil economies are willing to work across regional lines.
    - B Oil reserves are closely correlated with physical geography.
    - C The Middle East is the most highly developed region of Asia.
    - D OPEC members are engaged in a rivalry with other oil producers.

13. Iraq and Iran went to war against each other in the late 20th century. Iraq later invaded Kuwait. Based on this map, which is the most likely reason for these conflicts?
    - A Kuwait wished to withdraw from OPEC membership.
    - B Control of oil production sites was central to Iraq's economy.
    - C Iran opposed the political leaders of Iraq and Kuwait.
    - D Oil production levels in sub-Saharan Africa were increasing quickly.

See page 37 for answers.

Unit Answer Key UNIT 1

Lesson 1
1. title
2. map key or map legend
3. scale
4. compass rose Review the first section of the lesson to find descriptions of each map feature. Practice identifying map features by reviewing maps you find in textbooks, online, or in newspapers or magazines. You can also practice your skills by making your own maps of your home, school, or neighborhood. Add to and label on your map each kind of map feature.
5. D. See the Test Strategy for more help on this item.
6. C. Consider the definition of each type of map. A road map shows a special kind of information—routes and road names or numbers. Thematic maps are used to show special kinds of information, so this is a thematic map.

Lesson 2
1. usual weather in a place over time
2. half of Earth
3. how many people live in a certain area of land
4. longitude line at 0°; all other meridians measured in relation to this line

   If you defined any of these terms incorrectly, review the lesson content carefully. Watch out for these common misunderstandings:

   - Weather and climate are not exactly the same. Remember that weather happens at a given moment, but climate refers to weather over time.
   - Hemi- is a word part meaning half. However, Earth has four hemispheres because some overlap.
   - Population measures the total number of people in a place. Population density specifically refers to the number of people within a certain area of land. Population density varies depending on how close together people live. Two places could have the same population but different population densities.

   - Latitude lines travel east–west around Earth. Longitude lines travel north–south around Earth.
5. B. Find the main question asked: How many miles are between Sydney and Brisbane? Use the map scale to measure the approximate number of miles between these two cities. Be careful to note the number of miles rather than kilometers.
6. D. Remember that longitude lines travel north–south, so choices A and B can be eliminated. Find Adelaide on the map. Compare its location to the longitude lines shown.
7. A. Physical geography often influences population density. Places with lots of cities probably have higher population densities. This suggests favorable geographic factors like flat lands. Be careful of choices like D that could be true but are not supported by evidence in the map.
8. B. See the Test Strategy for more help on this item.

Lesson 3
1. Possible response: Two examples of demographic statistics that could be on the test are birth rate and death rate.
   Go back to the first section of the lesson. Review the information about population or demographic statistics.
2. A geographic model offers a way to visually show abstract information. It makes geography more concrete. Review the information in the section "Geographic Models."
3. Dr. Lopez should use a concentric zone model. This model relates to the process of economic development and urban growth. It makes sense for Dr. Lopez to compare both cities to this model and then to each other. Review the information in the section "Geographic Models." Consider how each model could be applied. Population pyramids and the demographic transition model both relate to specific population characteristics. They do not fit with Dr. Lopez's study. The concentric zone model makes the most sense.

4. C. Consider the uses of this map. It shows infant mortality rate, which relates to health care for mothers and babies.
5. A. Be careful not to make too big a leap in logic. The map shows variation in infant mortality rates across the country. Although this rate may be correlated with other characteristics, the only choice that is directly supported by the map is A.
6. A. See the Test Strategy for more help on this item.
7. D. This question is especially difficult. Find the main question asked—which state has the highest birth rate? Review the map. The map gives information about infant mortality rate but not about the overall number of births in a state. This information is related, but it cannot be determined from the map.

Lesson 4
1. D. See the Test Strategy for more help on this item.
2. A. Review the map carefully to find the regions where Democrats had the most support. Be careful of answers that might be partially correct.
3. B. Be sure to choose an answer that is directly supported by the map. Don't make too big a leap in logic.
4. A. Recall that a trend is a pattern over time. Only one choice shows changes or continuities in ideas over time.

Unit Test
1. B.
2. C.
3. D.
4. B.
5. D.
6. A.
7. C.
8. C.
9. C.
10. A.
11. C.
12. A.
13. B.

Unit Glossary

- **birth rate** – number of people in a population who are born each year out of 1,000
- **climate** – usual weather in a place over time
- **climate change** – shifts in climate over time
- **climate map** – map that shows patterns in climate and weather
- **compass rose** – map feature showing location of north
- **concentric zone model** – geographic model showing typical patterns of urban land use
- **cultural diffusion** – spread of ideas and practices from place to place
- **death rate** – number of people in a population who die each year out of 1,000
- **demographics** – study of populations
- **demographic transition model** – geographic model tracing patterns of population growth
- **economic map** – map that shows economic information like the locations of resources
- **Equator** – the central line of latitude
- **hemisphere** – half of Earth
- **human geography** – the study of how people interact with broad regional systems
- **infant mortality rate** – number of babies who die before reaching age one out of 1,000 births
- **key** – map feature that shows each symbol and its meaning (also called map legend)
- **latitude** – imaginary line that circles Earth from east to west
- **legend** – map feature that shows each symbol and its meaning (also called map key)
- **life expectancy** – number of years an average person can expect to live
- **longitude** – imaginary line that circles Earth from north to south
- **map projection** – the way in which the round Earth is transferred to a flat map
- **Mercator projection** – common map projection that distorts scale far from the Equator
- **migration** – movement of people from place to place
- **physical geography** – study of Earth and its landforms, bodies of water, and physical systems
- **physical map** – map that shows information about landforms and bodies of water
- **political map** – map that shows borders and cities
- **population density** – a measure of how many people live within a set land area, like a square mile or square kilometer
- **population pyramid** – geographic model showing populations by age bands and gender
- **prime meridian** – the central line of longitude
- **scale** – map feature showing distance
- **thematic map** – map that shows information a particular subject, like voting patterns, sites of military conflicts, or population patterns
- **weather** – measure of the atmospheric conditions in a place at a certain time, such as temperature, wind, and precipitation

Study More!

UNIT 1

Skills: Analyzing Maps
- Gnomic and conic maps
- Topographical maps
- Contour lines
- Almanacs, atlases, and globes
- Additional types of map projections

Geography Basics
- Regions, including formal, functional, and perceptual regions
- Types of terrain, including plains, plateaus, and tropical forests
- Development and use of time zones

Geographic Statistics and Models
- Census and data collection methods
- Immigration rate
- Literacy rate
- Economic development growth models

Human Geography
- Political systems
- Gerrymandering
- Religious practices
- Industrialization
- Land use
- Urbanization
- Agriculture and food production

UNIT 2

History

Why study history? Historians seek to interpret the past in order to understand why the world is the way it is today. Less than 100 years ago, African Americans in many states were treated unfairly by the law. They could not vote in elections or attend the same schools as white students, among other restrictions. The Civil Rights Movement forced changes to end these practices. Historians still study the lasting effects of these laws. The HiSET® will ask you to think like a historian in order to analyze various historical sources. It will also ask you to look for connections among past events.

KEY WORDS

- abolish
- agriculture
- Articles of Confederation
- atomic bomb
- bias
- boycott
- Byzantine Empire
- caravel
- cash crop
- city-state
- Civil Rights Movement
- Cold War
- Compromise of 1850
- conquistadors
- constitution
- Continental Congress
- cuneiform
- Dark Ages
- Declaration of Independence
- democracy
- dynasty
- Equal Rights Amendment
- fact
- feminism
- Fugitive Slave Law
- Great Depression
- hieroglyphics
- Homestead Act
- hunter-gatherer
- imperialism
- industrialization
- irrigation
- isolationism
- Kansas-Nebraska Act
- labor specialization
- Manifest Destiny
- mercantilism
- Mesoamerica
- Middle Passage
- militarism
- Missouri Compromise
- muckraker
- nationalism
- Native Americans
- New Deal
- opinion
- Persian Gulf War
- popular sovereignty
- primary source
- Proclamation of 1763
- Progressive Era
- Reformation
- Renaissance
- republic
- secede
- secondary source
- sectionalism
- segregation
- self-government
- speculation
- Transcontinental Railroad
- Treaty of Versailles
- triangular trade
- urbanization
- War on Terror

World History: Pre-History and the Ancient World

UNIT 2 / LESSON 1

The Ancient World

Historians generally agree that humans first evolved in Africa millions of years ago. Early people were **hunter-gatherers** who survived by collecting wild plants and hunting animals or fish. Hunter-gatherers usually lived in small, mobile groups. Over time, **agriculture**, or farming, arose alongside hunting and gathering. Agriculture allowed people to grow food that could be saved up for later consumption. Historians believe farming arose in different regions of the world, including southwest Asia, China, and the Americas.

Agricultural regions were home to the first significant human civilizations. Farming generated food surpluses that allowed some people to have jobs other than producing food. People had many roles, from priest to merchant to government official. This division of labor is known as **labor specialization**. Farming thus allowed for the creation of sophisticated societies. Some societies grew to include large empires. These included Sumer, China, and India. Kings who inherited their positions from their ancestors often ruled these societies. These ruling families are known as **dynasties**.

Ancient societies changed as they developed new technology. Early humans had used simple tools. Over time, people learned how to make clay into pottery and how to form iron. They developed systems of writing that used symbols to represent sounds and ideas. **Cuneiform** writing was cut into clay tablets. Egyptians wrote using **hieroglyphics**, which showed ideas through pictures. Technology also allowed for the construction of massive temples and public buildings.

KEY WORDS

- agriculture
- cuneiform
- dynasty
- hieroglyphics
- hunter-gatherer
- labor specialization

Interpreting Sources: Ancient Egyptian Culture

Ancient Egyptian civilization spanned thousands of years. Regular flooding there allowed for seasonal agriculture. Its rulers used some of Egypt's resources to build huge tombs known as pyramids. They also engaged in trade and conquest.

> Ancient Egyptians developed a complex civilization along the Nile River. Egyptians believed their ruler, known as the pharaoh, connected the divine world of the gods to earthly matters. Egyptians had many gods, and these figures had both animal and human forms. Sometimes, Egyptian gods were drawn with both animal and human characteristics.

Read this text closely. You can determine that ancient Egypt was polytheistic, worshiping multiple gods. You can also learn how to identify depictions of ancient Egyptian gods and goddesses in visuals.

The test will not expect you to know **every** fact about history. Instead, you must read and interpret text and, sometimes, draw conclusions about photos or illustrations. This text and illustration both tell about ancient Egypt.

Notice the figures with both human and animal features. These likely depict Egyptian deities. Look closely at the symbols in the upper right. These are examples of Egyptian hieroglyphics.

41

UNIT 2 / LESSON 1

Lesson Practice

KEY POINT!

Ancient civilizations grew and changed due to improvements in food production and technology.

TEST STRATEGY

Read the question carefully to make sure you fully understand what it is asking. Question 4 asks you to make an inference about how historians work. Review the passage and look specifically for details that relate to how historians have learned about ancient China. Notice the details about archeological discoveries. Now, find the answer that connects to this information. Avoid choices that relate to other details in the passage but do not tell about the work of historians.

Complete the activities below to check your understanding of the lesson content.

Skills Practice

Read the text and study the illustration. Then choose the correct answer to each question.

The Chinese began producing bronze goods more than 3,500 years ago. Archeologists have discovered bronze pots and vessels dating to perhaps 1500 BCE at Po, the capital of the ancient Shang dynasty. Early pieces were cast using a clay or ceramic mold. Over time, Chinese artisans added decorations and inscriptions to simple vessels. Eventually, they were able to add detailed figures. Historians believe ancient Chinese rulers used these bronze pieces mostly in religious rituals.

1. This text seeks mostly to explain
   A the jobs of Chinese rulers.
   B Chinese religious practices.
   C the development of Chinese technology.
   D how Chinese artisans made vessels.

2. According to the passage, which of the following is true?
   A The Chinese were the first people to make bronze goods.
   B The complexity of Chinese technology increased over time.
   C Archeologists are uncertain of the uses of Chinese bronze wares.
   D Chinese rulers were also the head of the state religion.

3. Based on the passage, what was the most likely use of the artifact shown in the photograph?
   A religious ceremonies
   B household storage
   C palace decoration
   D trade goods

4. Which inference best explains why historians' understanding of ancient China has changed over time?
   A Improved technology allows historians to recreate ancient bronze goods.
   B Archeological discoveries add facts and details to the historical record.
   C New findings help historians translate previously unknown ancient writings.
   D Interest in ancient technology and societies has grown in recent years.

See page 91 for answers and help.

World History: Classical Civilizations

UNIT 2 / LESSON 2

KEY WORDS
- city-state
- democracy
- republic

The Classical World

Classical civilizations arose around the world. Two of the best-known classical civilizations grew near the Mediterranean Sea. Ancient Greece was a collection of **city-states** with shared cultural characteristics. A city-state is an independent city with its own government and citizenship. Athens and Sparta were the leading Greek city-states. Sparta was a strong military power. Athens was a cultural and economic hub where the system of **democracy** first emerged. Democracy is a political system in which citizens vote directly on leaders and laws.

Ancient Greece flourished in the 400s and 300s BCE. During this time, the Roman Republic was growing on the nearby Italian peninsula. In a **republic**, citizens vote for leaders who then make laws on their behalf. During the 40s BCE, a Roman general named Julius Caesar became the sole leader of the republic. Some Romans worried he wished to be king, so they assassinated him. A period of turmoil followed. Caesar's adopted son, Augustus, became Rome's new leader. He is considered the first leader of the Roman Empire. The empire lasted for more than 400 years and included much of western Europe, northern Africa, and the eastern Mediterranean at its peak.

China also flourished during this time. The Han dynasty controlled China from about 200 BCE to the 200s CE. The Han supported the arts and culture, including sculpture, building, and poetry. Han leaders also encouraged technological developments, such as paper. During the Han dynasty, Buddhism arrived in China from India.

UNIT 2 / LESSON 2

Lesson Practice

Complete the activities below to check your understanding of the lesson content.

KEY POINT!

Classical civilizations developed in places like Greece, Rome, and China. They advanced government, culture, and technology.

Skills Practice

Read the text. Then choose the correct answer to each question.

Christianity began in the first century CE in the eastern Mediterranean. The faith is based on the life and teachings of a Jewish resident of Israel named Jesus. Historians agree that Jesus was a real person who was executed by the ruling Roman government in about 30 CE. However, they are uncertain about the exact origins of the four Gospels that spread Jesus' teachings.

Christianity became popular in the Roman Empire. But not all Romans accepted its teachings. Some Roman rulers, such as Nero, actively blamed Christians for Rome's problems. The emperor Constantine converted to Christianity and, in the 300s, made it illegal to persecute Christians. The Romans helped spread Christianity across Europe and into Asia. Today, Christianity is the most widely practiced religion worldwide.

TEST STRATEGY

Sometimes, questions that ask about specific ideas, like in Question 2, can be answered more easily before you read the answer choices. Practice this skill by covering the answer choices with your hand as you read each question. Then, come up with your own response. Read through the answer choices and pick the one closest to your own response.

1. Which conclusion is supported by the text?
   A Roman emperors opposed Christianity because it weakened their own standing.
   B The modern popularity of Christianity is at least partly a legacy of the Roman Empire.
   C Most Jews living in Israel in the first century converted to Christianity.
   D Historians believe that the writings of the Gospels are mostly fictional accounts.

2. Based on this passage, what generalization can be made about early Christianity?
   A The popularity of Christianity grew over time.
   B Few people listened to Jesus' teachings during his lifetime.
   C Early Christians sought to leave the Roman Empire.
   D Most followers of early Christianity were peasants.

3. Which of the following is the main historical source of information about Jesus' teachings?
   A Jewish records from Israel
   B books written by Constantine
   C writings of the emperor Nero
   D stories in the four Gospels

4. What inference about the relationship between Christianity and Judaism is best supported by this passage?
   A Christianity built on ideas present in Judaism.
   B Christianity completely replaced Judaism in Israel.
   C Judaism emerged in response to Christian teachings.
   D Judaism gained popularity as Romans persecuted Christians.

See page 91 for answers and help.

Fact and Opinion

UNIT 2 / LESSON 3

Determining Fact and Opinion

Historical sources often contain both **facts** and **opinions**. A fact is a statement that can be proven true. *The American Civil War began in 1861* is a fact. You can prove this statement true by researching it in a history book or encyclopedia. An opinion, on the other hand, gives a person's own beliefs about a topic. An opinion cannot be proven true or false. *The American Civil War was a terrible tragedy* is an opinion. It gives a judgment about the topic but cannot be definitely proven true or false.

Review some examples of facts and opinions:

Fact	Opinion
George Washington was the first U.S. president.	George Washington was the best U.S. president.
Austin is the capital of Texas.	Austin is the most dynamic city in Texas.
The governor proposed a new policy in a recent speech.	Voters should oppose the new policy proposed by the governor.

Follow these steps to tell the difference between facts and opinions:

Step 1: Read the statement. Identify its main point or claim.

Step 2: Ask, Can this point be proven definitely true or false? Or does it tell a belief or judgment?

Step 3: If you are unsure, look for clue words like could, should, feel, think, or believe. These words often indicate that the ideas that follow are opinions. Words like best or worst also often indicate opinions.

KEY WORDS

- fact
- opinion

UNIT 2 / LESSON 3

Lesson Practice

Complete the activities below to check your understanding of the lesson content.

Skills Practice

Read the text below from a 1969 speech given by U.S. President Richard Nixon. Then answer the questions that follow.

> Tonight I want to talk to you on a subject of deep concern to all Americans and to many people in all parts of the world—the war in Vietnam.
>
> I believe that one of the reasons for the deep division about Vietnam is that many Americans have lost confidence in what their Government has told them about our policy. The American people cannot and should not be asked to support a policy which involves the overriding issues of war and peace unless they know the truth about that policy.
>
> . . . Now, let me begin by describing the situation I found when I was inaugurated on January 20:
>
> — The war had been going on for 4 years. 1,000 Americans had been killed in action.
>
> — The training program for the South Vietnamese was behind schedule. 540,000 Americans were in Vietnam with no plans to reduce the number.
>
> — No progress had been made at the negotiations in Paris, and the United States had not put forth a comprehensive peace proposal.
>
> — The war was causing deep division at home and criticism from many of our friends as well as our enemies abroad.
>
> In view of these circumstances, there were some who urged that I end the war at once by ordering the immediate withdrawal of all American forces.

1. Based on the passage, which of the following is true?
   A   President Nixon opposed the Vietnam War.
   B   U.S. leaders mostly saw the war as a way to fight communism.
   C   The Vietnam War began in 1955.
   D   U.S. citizens disagreed about whether the war was justified.

2. Which of the following gives an opinion?
   A   Tonight I want to talk to you on . . . the war in Vietnam.
   B   The American people cannot and should not be asked to support a policy. . . .
   C   The war had been going on for 4 years.
   D   . . . the United States had not put forth a comprehensive peace proposal.

See page 91 for answers and help.

KEY POINT!

A fact is a statement that can proven true. An opinion is a statement that gives someone's ideas or beliefs.

TEST STRATEGY

A question that asks you to find a fact or opinion can be answered by asking yourself whether each choice is true or false. If you can definitely state that something is true or false, it must be a fact. If the choice could be either true or false depending on your interpretation, then it is more likely an opinion.

World History: The Early Modern Period

KEY WORDS
- Byzantine Empire
- Dark Ages
- Reformation
- Renaissance

The Dark Ages

After the fall of the Roman Empire, Europe was in disarray. No strong central government emerged to unify the area as the Roman Empire had. Local and regional lords controlled relatively small groups of people. They fought often. Cities declined. Interest in culture and learning became limited to a small group of elites. Little recorded history survives from this time period, which stretches from about 500 to 1000 CE. As a result, historians sometimes call it the **Dark Ages**.

At the same time, the **Byzantine Empire** based at Constantinople flourished. This empire had once been part of the Roman Empire. The emperor Constantine had established this area as the Eastern Roman Empire in the 300s, and it was ruled by a separate government using Roman methods. Under Emperor Justinian I, the Byzantine government created an important formal law code. Justinian also built the famous Hagia Sophia church. The Byzantine Empire survived until 1453.

Cultural and Religious Changes

After the Dark Ages, Western Europe underwent a period of regrowth. New agricultural tools and crops allowed for increased food yields and better nutrition. The European population grew as a result. Cities began to develop as economic centers of trade and commerce. People built town squares, roads, and cathedrals. Trade networks like the Silk Roads connected Europe with the Middle East and Asia, allowing new ideas to flow westward.

Beginning in the 1400s, a flowering of culture known as the **Renaissance** spread across parts of Europe. At the same time, people began to question traditional ways of thinking. They developed a scientific method that sought to explain the world through observation and experimentation. People also questioned the authority of the Catholic Church. German priest Martin Luther sparked a religious reform movement called the **Reformation**. The Reformation allowed for the development of many new Christian sects across Europe.

UNIT 2 / LESSON 4

World History: The Early Modern Period

Interpreting Sources: The Hundred Years' War

During the Middle Ages and early modern period, Europeans frequently went to war. They sought to control lands. They also wanted political power. After the Reformation, groups of differing religious denominations also fought. Disputes over political and religious matters resulted in conflicts like the Hundred Years' War.

> The Hundred Years' War was a lengthy series of conflicts between England and France. The war mostly took place between 1337 and 1453. However, tensions between the two countries extended beyond these time periods.
>
> By the 1300s, the English had many land claims on the European mainland. The English sought to expand their control over France. When the French throne became empty in 1328, both English and French leaders tried to claim it. French nobles wanted to give the throne to the French leader, Philip VI. Philip VI soon tried to retake French lands controlled by England, however, and war began.
>
> Fighting took place across northern France. Often, English armies launched drawn-out attacks known as sieges on French towns. The French people resisted these attacks. They did not want an English kind of France. A few times, England withdrew its claims. However, fighting always started again. The conflict went on until popular French resistance showed England that they could not control the land. As a result of the war, England withdrew almost entirely from mainland Europe. France became more united as a nation.

The introduction of this passage names its overall topic, the Hundred Years' War. You can infer that the passage will mostly seek to inform you about this time in world history.

Look for clue words to help you determine the sequence of events in this passage. The paragraph tells you that England had land claims by the 1300s. *Notice other specific years named in the paragraph. Look, too, for time and sequence words like* soon.

Practice ordering events based on the passage. What event happened before England gave up its claims to the French throne? The French people resisted. What event happened afterward? England mostly withdrew from mainland Europe.

Lesson Practice

UNIT 2 / LESSON 4

Complete the activities below to check your understanding of the lesson content.

Apply Your Knowledge

Read the text. Then choose the correct answer to each question.

The following excerpts are from the Magna Carta. King John of England agreed to the Magna Carta in 1215.

> TO ALL FREE MEN OF OUR KINGDOM we have also granted, for us and our heirs for ever, all the liberties written out below, to have and to keep for them and their heirs, of us and our heirs . . .
>
> (39) No free man shall be seized or imprisoned, or stripped of his rights or possessions, or outlawed or exiled, or deprived of his standing in any way, nor will we proceed with force against him, or send others to do so, except by the lawful judgment of his equals or by the law of the land.
>
> (40) To no one will we sell, to no one deny or delay right or justice.

1. Which right is guaranteed by the Magna Carta?
   - A freedom from slavery
   - B freedom of speech
   - C right to vote
   - D trial by jury

2. What inference about medieval England is best supported by this text?
   - A English people all had citizenship rights.
   - B King John was a strong and powerful king.
   - C English laws were not applied equally before 1215.
   - D Few crimes were committed during this time period.

TEST STRATEGY

Try to rewrite difficult questions to determine exactly what they ask. You might rewrite Question 2, for example, as *What does this passage suggest about England?* Then, review the answer choices. The text says that people cannot be punished for crimes unlawfully. This idea most connects to choice C.

UNIT 2 / LESSON 4

KEY POINT!

The fall of the Roman Empire began the Dark Ages. The growth of cities, commerce, and learning beginning in the 1000s pushed Europe toward modern times.

Lesson Practice

Skills Practice

Read the passage. Then place the events on the timeline in the correct order.

Leonardo da Vinci is considered one of the finest minds of the Renaissance. He was born in Italy in 1452. He is remembered partly as a scientist, sculptor, and architect, but as a young man he trained only to become a painter. Da Vinci's most famous paintings were the mural The Last Supper (1495–1498) and the portrait Mona Lisa (1503–1506), which is now displayed in Paris.

After 1500, da Vinci became interested in drafting, mathematics, and science. He recorded a series of scientific observations on topics like the human body, plant structure, and avian flight. In 1513, da Vinci left Florence for Rome, and three years later he moved to France. He worked for the French king until his death in 1519.

3. Add these events to the timeline in the correct sequence:

   Leonardo da Vinci paints *The Last Supper*

   The *Mona Lisa* is displayed in Paris

   Leonardo da Vinci trains as a painter

   Leonardo da Vinci makes scientific observations

See page 91 for answers and help.

World History: A Globalized World

UNIT 2 / LESSON 5

Exploration and Imperialism

Beginning in the 1400s, European interest in the broader world grew. Improved technology like the light, mobile ship called the **caravel** supported these aims. Portuguese navigators explored the coast of Africa seeking new trade routes to Asia. Italian navigator Christopher Columbus won the support of Spain to try a different route. He sailed west hoping to circle Earth and reach East Asia. Instead, he landed in the West Indies. Columbus's tale of the Americas sparked European exploration and conquest in the region. Spain, Portugal, France, England, and the Netherlands all set up land claims in the Americas. European conquest, diseases, and practices dramatically reduced native populations. European colonization also caused great numbers of Africans to be enslaved and brought forcibly to work in the Americas.

European interests in the Americas declined by the 1800s. Powerful European countries then began practicing **imperialism** in Africa and Asia. Imperialism is the use of power by one country to rule another.

The Industrialized World

Technology changed how people made goods. **Industrialization**, or the making of goods in factories, began during the 1700s and 1800s. Industrialization created jobs in factories. It led to the growth of cities near factories. The growth of cities is called **urbanization**. Cities had both their benefits and problems. They allowed for the development of a larger middle class. They had mass transportation, recreation opportunities, and many services. But, they also had overcrowding, disease, and crime.

Improved technology also caused destruction. World War I and World War II left a huge number of casualties. The United States used a powerful new weapon, the **atomic bomb**, against two Japanese cities in 1945. Fears of nuclear warfare shaped global relations after that time.

KEY WORDS

- atomic bomb
- caravel
- imperialism
- industrialization
- mercantilism
- Middle Passage
- triangular trade
- urbanization

World History: A Globalized World

Interpreting Sources: Triangular Trade

European colonization of the Americas led to the establishment of a **triangular trade**. This was a set of routes connecting the Americas, Europe, and West Africa. It carried raw materials, finished goods, and enslaved Africans across the Atlantic Ocean. The route from Africa to the Americas carried millions of enslaved people as ship cargo. This long and difficult journey is known as the **Middle Passage**.

European countries like England used an economic theory called mercantilism. Under this theory, colonies existed to supply raw materials to their ruling countries. They also acted as markets to buy that country's finished goods.

The Triangular Trade

> The triangular trade created a globalized economy in the Atlantic. Study the overall shape of the trade routes shown on this map. Why do you think this system is called the triangular trade?

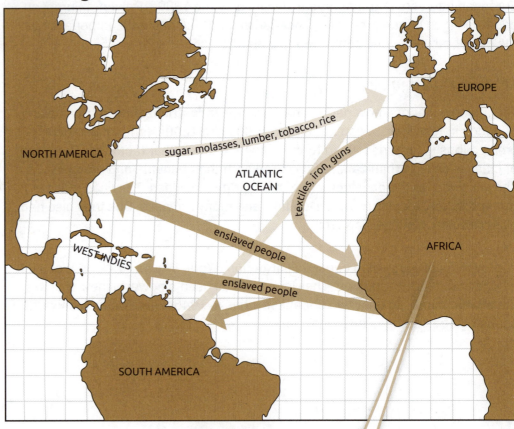

> The forced movement of Africans to the Americas was one of the largest migrations in history. Millions of Africans arrived in the Caribbean, Brazil, and the southeastern region of North America. Slavery was a main labor system in all of these areas into the 1800s.

Lesson Practice

UNIT 2 / LESSON 5

Complete the activities below to check your understanding of the lesson content.

Vocabulary

Write definitions in your own words for each of the key terms.

1. imperialism _____
   _____

2. industrialization _____
   _____

3. mercantilism _____
   _____

4. Middle Passage _____
   _____

5. triangular trade _____
   _____

6. urbanization _____
   _____

KEY POINT!

Exploration, imperialism, and industrialization all helped link the world's economies and societies.

UNIT 2 / LESSON 5 — Lesson Practice

TEST STRATEGY

Be sure to carefully read the test question to make sure you find the right information. Question 9 asks you to find the regions with the *least*, or *lowest*, number of arrivals. Choice D gives the two regions with the *greatest* number of arrivals. Reading the question too quickly could cause you to mistake this for the right answer.

Apply Your Knowledge

Review the graph. Then choose the correct answer to each question.

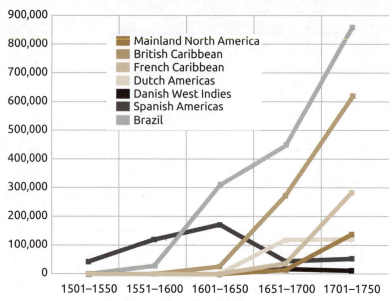

Source: Emory University, Trans-Atlantic Slave Trade Database

7. Which region had the most enslaved people arrive after 1600?
   A Brazil
   B British Caribbean
   C Mainland North America
   D Spanish Americas

8. Which reason most likely explains the number of enslaved people arriving in mainland North America before 1600?
   A The development of the cotton gin reduced the need for enslaved labor.
   B Most colonies in the region had laws banning slavery.
   C Very few European settlements existed in the region during this time.
   D European countries struggled with Native Americans for control of the region.

9. Which two regions received the least number of enslaved people during the period 1651–1700?
   A Brazil and British Caribbean
   B British Caribbean and French Caribbean
   C Mainland North America and the Danish West Indies
   D Spanish Americas and Brazil

See page 91 for answers and help.

Reliability of Sources

UNIT 2 / LESSON 6

KEY WORDS

- bias
- primary source
- secondary source

Evaluating Historical Sources

To understand an event or a trend, historians draw on different sources. They may use **primary sources**, which are people who witnessed an event. Primary sources often include newspaper articles, diaries, public records, photographs, and letters. Historians also use **secondary sources**. These sources were created by someone who did not witness the event described. Common secondary sources are encyclopedias, journal articles, and books.

An important part of analyzing both primary and secondary sources is determining whether they are reliable. A reliable source is one that can be trusted to provide accurate and trustworthy information. Usually, reliable sources are free of **bias**. A bias is a personal opinion that shapes how someone views a topic.

Both primary and secondary sources can be reliable. Reliable primary sources give facts and details about what really happened in the past. A newspaper article telling what happened at a past event, for example, is usually a reliable source. A letter written by someone who just heard about that event might be unreliable, however, because the author does not have direct knowledge of what happened. Reliable secondary sources are often written by experts. Historical books, articles, and encyclopedias are usually reliable. A blog post or a school paper is more likely to be unreliable.

Ask the following questions to help determine whether a source is reliable. Not every question will apply to every source.

- Who is the author or creator of the source? When was it created?
- What is the author's purpose in creating this source? Is it to give facts and information, or is it to persuade someone to agree with his or her point of view?
- What qualifications does the author have to tell about this topic?
- Does the author tell how he or she gathered information for this source? Is there a bibliography or list of works cited?

UNIT 2 / LESSON 6

Lesson Practice

Complete the activities below to check your understanding of the lesson content.

Skills Practice

Read the text below. Then choose the correct answer to each question or write complete sentences in response.

Source X

Historians have identified many factors that weakened the Roman Empire. Its vast territories were difficult for a single ruler to oversee. German invasions along its borders further weakened its hold on these lands. Political corruption hurt the empire from within. Leaders could not command loyalty from their citizens or, most importantly, their armies. The slow decline of the empire led to its fall in 476 when a German invader took the imperial throne.

—*from* A Brief Guide to Roman History, *by Dr. Eminent, Professor of Classical History, Community University*

Source Y

Rome was guaranteed to fall as soon as it became an empire. It was too big, and its leaders were too greedy. Julius Caesar was a skilled general but a terrible politician. He won elections by bribing voters and pressuring them into voting for him. Later emperors followed his example. When invaders finally overthrew the last emperor in 476, it was for the good of the Roman people.

from Mark's Roman History Blog, published April 4, 2002

1. What is the main topic of both sources?
   - A   the life of Julius Caesar
   - B   the decline of the Roman Empire
   - C   Roman military strategy
   - D   ways of life in ancient Rome

2. Which is true of Source X?
   - A   It was written by an expert.
   - B   It seeks mostly to persuade readers.
   - C   It is a primary source.
   - D   It has an obvious bias.

3. Which source is more reliable? How can you tell?

   _____
   _____
   _____
   _____

See page 91 for answers and help.

KEY POINT!

Reliable sources are written by experts or others who are well informed about a topic.

TEST STRATEGY

Questions that ask you to find statements that are accurate or true are best addressed by using the process of elimination. Read each answer choice. Mark it out if it makes a claim that is not correct. Question 2 gives several possible characteristics of Source X. You can tell that Choice C is not correct, for example, because the source is a book, which is a secondary source. Which other choices can you eliminate?

U.S. History: Pre-Columbian Americas

UNIT 2 / LESSON 7

KEY WORDS

- irrigation
- Mesoamerica
- Native Americans

Settlement of the Americas

Historians generally agree that humans arrived in the Americas between 20,000 and 60,000 years ago. People likely crossed over the Bering Strait on a land bridge. During colder times, the freezing of nearby water revealed a pathway connecting Asia and what is now Alaska. As Earth warmed, melting glaciers covered this path. Smaller numbers of people may have arrived later in boats across the Pacific.

The earliest Americans were hunter-gatherers. They spread southward following animals and gathering plants. Over time, they reached what is now Central and South America. Estimates of the total American population vary. Perhaps 5.5 to 20 million people lived in the Americas by the late 1400s.

North American Civilizations

Historians call the groups who lived in what is now the United States **Native Americans**. These peoples had different ways of life. Most relied on simple farming techniques to produce at least some of their food. People in the dry Southwest developed **irrigation** systems to move water to croplands. Groups near rivers and oceans fished.

The Mississippian culture built the largest city in North America. It was called Cahokia. This city flourished between about 950 and 1350. Cahokia was home to perhaps 20,000 people at its height.

Mesoamerican Civilizations

Historians often refer to the region of Mexico, Central America, and South America as **Mesoamerica**. Mesoamericans developed agriculture independently. They created settled societies. Historians have learned about their ways of life from written records, oral traditions, artifacts, and structures.

The most significant Mesoamerican civilizations were the Inca, the Maya, and the Aztec. The Inca controlled large territories along the Andes Mountains. They had a centralized government and extensive road network. The Aztec had a military empire centered on the city of Tenochtitlan. When the Spanish conquered the Aztec, they made this site their own capital, called Mexico City.

UNIT 2 / LESSON 7

U.S. History: Pre-Columbian Americas

Interpreting Sources: Mayan Technology

The Maya lived across parts of what is now Mexico, Guatemala, and Belize. The earliest Mayan settlements existed by 1500 BCE. The Maya flourished between about 250 CE and 900 CE. They built large cities, like Chichen Itza. Although the Mayan civilization declined after 900, Mayans still live in Mexico and Central America today. About 5 million people speak Mayan languages in this region.

> The first paragraph tells what the main topic of this passage is. It also points out the differences and similarities between Mayan and modern times. Mayans did not have modern technology.

The achievements of Mayan technology continue to fascinate people today. Mayans did not have modern machines or tools. But they were able to make great advances. Long ago, the Mayans quarried huge limestone rocks. They used these to construct temples and public buildings like ball courts and markets.

Mayan astronomers and mathematicians were very skilled. They developed an accurate, 365-day calendar based on the rotation of Earth around the Sun. They noted the movement of bodies like the Moon and Venus. They could even predict when solar eclipses would occur.

> Find the main idea of this paragraph: *Mayan astronomers and mathematicians were very skilled.* Notice that the rest of the paragraph gives specific details and examples to support this idea.

Mayans also developed the most thorough writing system in Mesoamerica. Like ancient Egyptians, they used pictures called hieroglyphs to represent sounds, objects, or ideas. Most Mayan symbols show everyday items. Mayans wrote inscriptions on slabs, buildings, and pottery. They also gathered writings in books called codices. Four Mayan codices survive today. Historians continue to work to understand this complex writing system.

> What do you already know about hieroglyphics? This paragraph defines this term. It gives details to further explain how hieroglyphics work to record language. Finally, it tells what makes Mayan hieroglyphics unique.

Lesson Practice

UNIT 2 / LESSON 7

Complete the activities below to check your understanding of the lesson content.

Apply Your Knowledge

Choose the correct answer to each question.

1. Which term best describes the earliest settlers of the Americas?
   A scientists
   B Europeans
   C farmers
   D hunter-gatherers

2. What problem caused Native Americans in the Southwest to develop irrigation systems?
   A They lived in a very dry climate.
   B They were far from Mayan civilization.
   C They practiced farming to get food.
   D They were unable to trade with Cahokia.

3. Which region did the Inca control?
   A Mexico, Guatemala, and Belize
   B area near the Andes Mountains
   C Mississippi River valley
   D area near what is now Mexico City

4. Based on the information in this lesson, what conclusion about Mesoamerican societies is best supported?
   A They were less advanced than North American societies.
   B They did not know that other civilizations existed nearby.
   C They lacked the weapons and power needed to defeat the Spanish.
   D They put most of their resources into surviving and growing food.

TEST STRATEGY

If you are unsure about the correct answer, try testing each choice to see if it is true or false. Review the answer choices for Question 4. The lesson tells about many achievements of Mesoamerican civilizations, so Choice A is false. The lesson states that the Inca built roads, which suggests that Choice B is also false. However, the lesson says that the Aztec were defeated by the Spanish. Choice C is true. What do you think about Choice D?

UNIT 2 / LESSON 7

Lesson Practice

KEY POINT!

People settled the Americas long ago. Native Americans lived mostly in small groups. Mesoamericans built large and complex civilizations.

Skills Practice

Add causes or effects to the chart based on the lesson content.

Cause	Effect
5. _____	People crossed over the Bering Strait land bridge.
People in the Southwest developed irrigation systems.	6. _____
The Inca needed to reach places across their empire.	7. _____

See page 91 for answers and help.

U.S. History: Colonization and Settlement

UNIT 2 / LESSON 8

KEY WORDS

- cash crop
- conquistadors
- self-government

Conquest and Exploration

European explorers arrived in the Americas soon after Columbus's expedition in 1492. Spanish **conquistadors** were adventurers and conquerors. Conquistadors like Hernán Cortés overcame native empires and spread European land claims. European settlement was at first focused mostly on the Caribbean, Central America, and parts of South America.

European explorers reached North America in the late 1400s. John Cabot explored the northeastern coast of North America on behalf of England. Spanish explorer Hernando de Soto was the first European to map territory along the Mississippi River. The Spanish established the first permanent European settlement in North America at St. Augustine, Florida, in 1565.

Spread of European Settlement

The English claimed lands throughout the eastern half of North America. Some of these colonies—often called the "Thirteen Colonies"—later formed the United States. Others became part of Canada. During much of the colonial era, France, Spain, and the Netherlands also had land claims in the area. The French, for example, claimed Quebec and other lands east of the Mississippi River until the 1760s. The Dutch settled the city of New Amsterdam, which became New York. Spain claimed territory in Florida and the Southwest.

Jamestown, Virginia, was the first successful permanent English settlement in North America. The Pilgrims founded the colony of Plymouth in 1620. They agreed to form themselves into a civil unit for the purposes of governing the colony. Historians see this as the first time Americans practiced **self-government**. Self-government is the overseeing of a community's political affairs by its own representatives.

UNIT 2 / LESSON 8

U.S. History: Colonization and Settlement

Interpreting Sources: Three Colonial Regions

The colonies that became the United States stretched across what is now Maine in the north to Georgia and South Carolina in the south. Historians often organize the colonies into three regions: New England, the Middle Colonies, and the Southern Colonies. New England lacked good soil but had long coastlines and rich forests. The Middle Colonies were the colonial breadbasket and were more ethnically and religiously diverse than other regions. The Southern Colonies practiced mostly **cash crop** agriculture. Cash crops are crops, like tobacco and cotton, grown mostly for sale. Southern farms needed lots of laborers, so slavery became important in the region.

> You will likely see questions asking you to compare and contrast features shown on a map. Study the New England and Southern Colonies. You can determine that they are similar in sharing long coastlines. You can conclude that they probably had different climates because of their locations.

American Colonies

> Remember to review the map legend and title in order to figure out what it shows. This map shows the three colonial regions in what became the United States.

> The text you just read described the Middle Colonies as the colonial breadbasket. Consider how the Middle Colonies' location might have contributed to this. It was probably easy to ship goods both north and south because of its central location. The Middle Colonies also had good water connections for trade.

Labels on map: New Hampshire, Massachusetts, New York, Rhode Island, Connecticut, Pennsylvania, New Jersey, Delaware, Virginia, Maryland, North Carolina, South Carolina, Georgia

Legend:
- New England
- Middle Colonies
- Southern Colonies

Scale: 0–400 km / 0–400 mi

Lesson Practice

UNIT 2 / LESSON 8

Complete the activities below to check your understanding of the lesson content.

Apply Your Knowledge

Choose the correct answer to each question.

1. What was the main goal of the conquistadors?
   - A to explore and claim land
   - B to create permanent settlements
   - C to trade with native peoples
   - D to build farms and sell crops

2. What was the first permanent settlement in North America?
   - A Jamestown
   - B New Amsterdam
   - C Plymouth
   - D St. Augustine

3. Which of the following is an example of cash crop agriculture?
   - A A community sets up a shared garden space.
   - B A trader buys and sells cloth made from cotton.
   - C A small farmer plants tomatoes, squash, and corn.
   - D A plantation grows large amounts of rice to sell for profits.

4. New England had fewer enslaved Africans than other colonial regions. Which fact most likely explains this condition?
   - A New England was first settled by Pilgrims.
   - B The Middle Colonies were ethnically and religiously diverse.
   - C New England's rocky soil was not very good for growing crops.
   - D The Southern Colonies were more sparsely populated than other regions.

TEST STRATEGY

To answer questions that ask for examples, begin by defining the most important word or phrase. Question 3 asks for an example of cash crop agriculture. First, define *cash crop agriculture*: farming crops for profits. Now review the answer choices. Which one is the best example of this definition?

Lesson 8 / U.S. History: Colonization and Settlement

UNIT 2 / LESSON 8

Lesson Practice

KEY POINT!

Europeans settled all across the Americas after 1492. The English claimed a great deal of land in North America.

Skills Practice

Reread the following text from the lesson. Then write complete sentences to answer the questions that follow.

> New England lacked good soil but had long coastlines and rich forests. The Middle Colonies were the colonial breadbasket and were more ethnically and religiously diverse than other regions. The Southern Colonies mostly practiced cash crop agriculture. Cash crops are crops, like tobacco and cotton, grown mostly for sale. Southern farms needed lots of laborers, so slavery became important in the region.

5. What was one way in which the Middle Colonies and Southern Colonies were similar?

   _____

   _____

6. What was one way in which New England was unlike the Middle Colonies and Southern Colonies?

   _____

   _____

7. Which two regions were most alike? Explain your answer.

   _____

   _____

   _____

   _____

See page 91 for answers and help.

U.S. History: The Early Republic

American Revolution

Competition between the British and French over American land contributed to the outbreak of the French and Indian War. Britain and its American colonists fought France and its Native American allies from 1754 to 1763. Britain gained lands from France as a result of the war. But the conflict was costly, and Britain hoped to avoid future conflicts. The **Proclamation of 1763** set a western limit for British colonial settlement. Britain also placed new taxes on the colonies to help pay for the war.

These policies angered many colonists. They resisted British taxes by **boycotting**, or refusing to buy, certain British goods. Because the colonists lacked a voice in Parliament, they argued that they were subject to "taxation without representation." Tensions rose during the 1760s and early 1770s. British and American soldiers fought at Lexington and Concord in 1775. The next year, a gathering of colonial leaders decided to declare independence from Great Britain. Fighting continued until 1781. The Treaty of Paris officially gave the United States independence in 1783.

A New Nation

The first U.S. government was set up under the **Articles of Confederation**. The Articles gave most powers to the states. Congress passed the Northwest Ordinances, a series of laws that organized western territories, like Ohio and Wisconsin. It lacked power to manage the nation's finances, however, and struggled to respond to problems. The weaknesses of the Articles led U.S. leaders to meet in Philadelphia to revise them in 1787. Instead, they wrote a new plan for government: the U.S. **Constitution**. It was ratified in 1789 after much debate.

During the early 1800s, a spirit of **nationalism** swept the country. Nationalism is support for one's own nation above others. National leaders pushed for the development of a transportation system to link the states together. Roads and canals encouraged trade and economic growth.

KEY WORDS

- Articles of Confederation
- boycott
- constitution
- Continental Congress
- Declaration of Independence
- nationalism
- Proclamation of 1763

U.S. History: The Early Republic

Interpreting Sources: Declaration of Independence

Colonial leaders gathered at two major meetings in the 1770s. At these gatherings, the **Continental Congress** set American policy. It also made decisions about the war with Great Britain. The Second Continental Congress issued the **Declaration of Independence**. Written mostly by Thomas Jefferson, this document announced that the British king had gone against the natural rights of the colonists.

> IN CONGRESS, July 4, 1776.
>
> The unanimous Declaration of the thirteen united States of America,
>
> When in the Course of human events, it becomes necessary for one people to dissolve the political bands which have connected them with another, and to assume among the powers of the earth, the separate and equal station to which the Laws of Nature and of Nature's God entitle them, a decent respect to the opinions of mankind requires that they should declare the causes which impel them to the separation.
>
> We hold these truths to be self-evident, that all men are created equal, that they are endowed by their Creator with certain unalienable Rights, that among these are Life, Liberty and the pursuit of Happiness.--That to secure these rights, Governments are instituted among Men, deriving their just powers from the consent of the governed, --That whenever any Form of Government becomes destructive of these ends, it is the Right of the People to alter or to abolish it, and to institute new Government, laying its foundation on such principles and organizing its powers in such form, as to them shall seem most likely to effect their Safety and Happiness.

This paragraph tells the purpose of the document. The colonists think they have a duty to tell the British why they are declaring independence, or "the causes which impel them to the separation."

This statement connects to political ideas of the Enlightenment. Enlightenment thinkers stated the people had certain rights just by being human. Jefferson calls these "unalienable rights."

"Consent of the governed" is another Enlightenment idea. This principle states that citizens agree to give up some of their rights to the government for the good of society as a whole. The Declaration says that the British government is no longer good for American colonists, so they are taking back their consent.

Lesson Practice

UNIT 2 / LESSON 9

Complete the activities below to check your understanding of the lesson content.

Vocabulary

Write definitions in your own words for each of the key terms.

1. boycott _____
_____

2. constitution _____
_____

3. nationalism _____
_____

4. Proclamation of 1763 _____
_____

Apply Your Knowledge

Choose the correct answer to each question.

5. Which of these did NOT contribute to colonial anger at Great Britain during the 1760s and 1770s?
    A   the issuance of the Proclamation of 1763
    B   the holding of the Continental Congresses
    C   the placement of new taxes on the colonies
    D   the lack of colonial representation in Parliament

TEST STRATEGY

Occasionally, questions may include words like *not* or *least*. These questions require you to consider each choice to find the one that does not apply to the tested topic. Review Question 5. This question asks for something that did *not* contribute to colonial anger at Great Britain. Use the process of elimination to check each choice. One is an effect of colonial tensions rather than a cause.

UNIT 2 / LESSON 9

KEY POINT!

The United States won independence from Great Britain in the American Revolution. The new nation tried different plans for government and grew quickly.

Lesson Practice

6. What was one way in which the United States showed nationalism in the early 1800s?
    A by building a transportation network
    B by writing the U.S. Constitution
    C by signing the Treaty of Paris
    D by organizing a national government

7. Which of these was a main achievement of the U.S. government under the Articles of Confederation?
    A paying off the U.S. national debt
    B organizing Western lands
    C declaring independence from Britain
    D winning the French and Indian War

Skills Practice

Write complete sentences to answer the questions that follow.

8. Think about the policies given in the Proclamation of 1763 and the Northwest Ordinances. How did these show change over time?

   _____

   _____

9. Think about the Articles of Confederation and the U.S. Constitution. How do these show continuity, or similarity, over time?

   _____

   _____

10. What is one way in which the French and Indian War connects to today? Explain your answer.

    _____

    _____

    _____

    _____

See page 91 for answers and help.

U.S. History: Civil War and Industrialization

Development of Sectionalism

Sectionalism is support for one's own region rather than the nation as a whole. During the early 1800s, sectionalism became a serious problem in the United States. The North and South had great sectional differences. The North was becoming more industrial. The South still relied heavily on cash crop agriculture. Northerners had begun ending slavery in the late 1700s. Enslaved populations in the South were growing. Southerners were also angry at economic policies that they believed favored the North.

U.S. leaders took several measures to keep sectionalism from breaking the nation in two. The **Missouri Compromise** of 1820 admitted Missouri and Maine as states at the same time to keep the balance of slave and free states in the U.S. Senate. It also set a northern limit for the expansion of slavery. The Missouri Compromise settled tensions for a while. But westward growth and expansion fueled them again. The **Compromise of 1850** attempted to resolve the matter again. It admitted California as a free state. It organized Western territories and allowed some to use **popular sovereignty**—the vote—to decide the slavery question. It also created a law that required all citizens to help catch runaway slaves. This **Fugitive Slave Law** was very unpopular in the North.

Civil War and Reconstruction

Disagreements over slavery continued to grow worse. Sectionalism, slavery, and political disagreements contributed to the beginning of the Civil War in 1861. Eleven Southern states **seceded**, or left the United States, in late 1860 and 1861. These states formed the Confederate States of America. They thought they had the right to leave the nation since they had agreed to join it in the 1780s. U.S. leaders disagreed. The Union and Confederacy fought for four years to decide this question. The Union eventually won.

A period called Reconstruction followed the Civil War. During Reconstruction, the Southern states slowly rejoined the Union. U.S. leaders made them agree to **abolish**, or end, slavery forever. They also made them extend voting rights to African Americans and agree that they were U.S. citizens. For a short time, African Americans had a voice in state and national government. But as Reconstruction ended, new laws limited their rights. Southern laws permitted discrimination and **segregation**, or the legal separation of people by race.

Westward Expansion and Industrialization

The United States followed a policy known as **Manifest Destiny** during the 1800s. Manifest Destiny was the idea that the nation had a duty to cover the continent all the way to the Pacific Ocean. It spurred people to move west. So did discoveries of gold and other valuable resources in places like California and Nevada. Americans also settled in Mexican lands like Texas. Texans fought a war for independence in the 1830s and joined the United States in 1845. Soon after, the United States fought a border war with Mexico. It received huge areas of Western lands as a result.

KEY WORDS

- abolish
- Compromise of 1850
- Fugitive Slave Law
- Homestead Act
- Kansas-Nebraska Act
- Manifest Destiny
- Missouri Compromise
- popular sovereignty
- secede
- sectionalism
- segregation
- Transcontinental Railroad

U.S. History: Civil War and Industrialization

New technology encouraged industrialization throughout this time. Workers operated machines to make all kinds of goods. By the late 1800s, the perfection of steel-making technology and the discovery of oil grew industry further. Better transportation and communication inventions, such as the telephone, also encouraged economic growth.

Industrialization and immigration are closely connected. During the early and mid-1800s, many immigrants came to the United States from places like Germany and Ireland. Later in the century, more and more immigrants came from Eastern and Southern Europe, especially Italy. Immigrants provided labor in factories. So did native-born Americans who moved to growing cities from farms. Cities like New York, Chicago, and Detroit became industrial hubs.

Interpreting Sources: Caning of Charles Sumner

Charles Sumner was an anti-slavery Senator from Massachusetts. Throughout his career, he opposed measures to allow the expansion of slavery into newly organized territories and states. Sumner strongly spoke against both the Compromise of 1850 and the **Kansas-Nebraska Act**. This act overturned the Missouri Compromise and permitted the expansion of slavery into the newly organized territories of Kansas and Nebraska. Sumner's attacks on the act included insults to the act's authors. Congressman Preston Brooks was the nephew of one of the authors of the bill. In May of 1856, he stormed into the Senate chambers and attacked Sumner with a cane. Sumner was severely injured and did not fully recover for years. The attack exemplified the extreme tension between North and South in this era.

Arguments of the Chivalry

> The quote by Henry Ward Beecher at the top of the political cartoon reads: *The symbol of the North is the pen; the symbol of the South is the bludgeon*. A bludgeon is a heavy stick or club used to injure others.

> Chivalry was a medieval code of honor used by knights. The artist uses the title ironically to suggest that the Southerners are acting in an immoral way. The text and images in this cartoon show a clearly Northern point of view on the events.

> The man writing is Charles Sumner. The man about to bring down the cane is Preston Brooks. Notice that Sumner is unarmed and unprepared to defend himself. Behind Brooks, another figure holds a club and a pistol to prevent the other Senators from stopping the attack.

U.S. History: Civil War and Industrialization

UNIT 2 / LESSON 10

Interpreting Sources: Native Americans and Westward Expansion

The **Homestead Act** of 1862 sped up the pace of American settlement in the West. The act gave people free land under certain conditions. A few years later, workers completed the first **Transcontinental Railroad** linking the nation from sea to sea. This further encouraged Americans to settle in Western lands that had previously been difficult to reach.

However, Native Americans already lived on these lands. White settlers pushed native people from their traditional homes and used resources on which Native Americans relied. Conflict was unavoidable. By the late 1800s, Native Americans were limited to reservations and had lost much of their culture.

The following quotation was spoken by a Kiowa chief named Santana in 1867.

> A long time ago this land belonged to our fathers; but when I go up to the river I see camps of soldiers here on its bank. These soldiers cut down my timber; they kill my buffalo; and when I see that, my heart feels like bursting; I feel sorry.

> *Santana expresses sadness at the changes in the West. His words show the Native American point of view on white settlement. He thinks it has hurt his people and the land.*

The following text is from a letter written by William Hornaday, an American hunter who traveled to the West in 1886 to collect bison hides for a museum exhibit.

> Dear Sir:
>
> Mr. Hadley and I with a Cheyenne Indian, White Dog, have just returned to camp from a five days scout through the bad lands, during which we camped beside our horses whenever night overtook us,—and we got an old bull buffalo day before yesterday. There were only two buffalo in that land (!), and we got the largest and finest one.
>
> Since seeing the buffalo on this native heath I am more than ever impressed with our wants in the way of good mountable skins of fine specimens, and still more of the imperative duty which devolves upon some institution to collect a store of skins to meet the demands of the future, when the bones of the last American bison shall lie bleaching on the prairie....

> *Think about how these points of view are similar and different. Both men are concerned about the changes to the Western landscape. Santana sees the changes as an end to his people's way of life. How does this differ from Hornaday's point of view?*

> *Hornaday is surprised by the decline in the number of buffalo he sees in the West. However, he hunts one for the exhibit. He also states that it is important for people to hunt and collect skins for museums to have.*

Lesson Practice

Complete the activities below to check your understanding of the lesson content.

Vocabulary

Complete each sentence with the correct key term from the bank.

| abolish | Fugitive Slave Law | Kansas-Nebraska Act | Manifest Destiny |
| popular sovereignty | secede | sectionalism | segregation |

1. The _____ was a controversial part of the Compromise of 1850.

2. The Missouri Compromise set a northern limit for slavery that the _____ overturned.

3. Eleven states decided to _____ from the United States in 1860 and 1861.

4. Voters using the idea of _____ decided whether to allow slavery in a territory.

5. During Reconstruction, Southern states had to agree to _____ slavery for good.

6. A belief in _____ encouraged many Americans to move west toward the Pacific Ocean.

7. Support for one's own region over the interest of the whole nation is called _____.

8. Southern laws allowed _____ after Reconstruction ended.

Lesson Practice

UNIT 2 / LESSON 10

Apply Your Knowledge

Choose the correct answer to each question.

9. What was the most important factor in the start of the Civil War?
    - A development of industry in the North
    - B caning of Charles Sumner by Preston Brooks
    - C disagreements over the expansion of slavery
    - D arrival of millions of immigrants to growing cities

10. Which of these states was admitted to the United States as a result of the Missouri Compromise?
    - A Maine
    - B Texas
    - C Kansas
    - D Nebraska

11. Which of these is an example of Manifest Destiny?
    - A States in New England abolished slavery.
    - B Chicago became an industrial center.
    - C South Carolina seceded from the United States.
    - D The United States annexed Texas.

12. What was one main problem of Reconstruction?
    - A It did not successfully readmit Confederate states.
    - B It temporarily ended westward expansion.
    - C It did not give freed slaves lasting rights.
    - D It failed to decide whether secession was legal.

13. Most immigrants to the United States in the late 1800s found work in
    - A rural farms.
    - B urban factories.
    - C the army.
    - D western gold mines.

TEST STRATEGY

Read the question carefully to find words like *most* or *greatest*. These often signal that you will need to evaluate the answer choices to make a judgment. Read Question 9. What do you think was the most important issue behind the Civil War? State your own answer to the question based on your reading. Then, evaluate each answer choice in Question 9. Choose the one that most closely matches your own idea.

UNIT 2 / LESSON 10

KEY POINT!

Slavery divided the United States during the early 1800s and eventually contributed to the Civil War. Westward expansion and industrialization reshaped the nation in the decades after the war ended.

Lesson Practice

Skills Practice

Study the sources. Then write complete sentences to answer the questions that follow.

This illustration from 1869 shows an official from the Freedmen's Bureau. The Freedmen's Bureau worked to help freed slaves in the South during the period of Reconstruction.

14. Which two main groups are shown in this illustration?

   _____

   _____

15. What are two issues about which these groups likely had different points of view?

   _____

   _____

Lesson Practice
UNIT 2 / LESSON 10

16. Does this illustrator think Reconstruction is a success? Explain your answer.

   _____

   _____

   _____

   _____

17. How might a former Confederate have reacted to this illustration? Explain your answer.

   _____

   _____

   _____

   _____

See page 92 for answers and help.

U.S. History: The 20th Century

KEY WORDS

- Civil Rights Movement
- Cold War
- Equal Rights Amendment
- feminism
- Great Depression
- isolationism
- militarism
- muckraker
- New Deal
- Progressive Era
- speculation
- Treaty of Versailles

World War I and World War II

World War I began in Europe in 1914. It resulted from growing regional competition and problems of nationalism and **militarism**. Militarism is a national focus on building military power. The United States had long followed a policy of **isolationism**, or staying out of global conflicts. Many Americans wanted to stay neutral in the war. But the United States entered the war in 1917. Germany had sent a message to Mexico that threatened U.S. interests. Leaders also worried about Germany's practice of sinking non-military ships in the Atlantic Ocean. U.S. troops helped win the war in 1919.

The **Treaty of Versailles** ending World War I hurt Germany badly. It also angered Italy, which felt that its wartime sacrifices went unrewarded. Powerful dictators rose in both these countries. German dictator Adolf Hitler blamed the Jews and other groups for Germany's problems. He began programs to harass and murder these people. He wanted to expand Germany across Europe. In 1939, his ambitions sparked World War II. Millions of people died in the war before it ended in 1945.

Great Depression and New Deal

The **Great Depression** was a worldwide economic downturn. The Depression had several causes. Americans had bought many goods on credit in the 1920s. New consumption slowed as people spent their money paying down debts. Stock **speculation** drove up stock prices in a bubble. Speculation is buying something in the hopes of selling it later for a higher price. Economic troubles in Europe weakened trade. In 1929, the U.S. stock market crashed. People worried about their savings and took their money out of banks. The situation quickly worsened.

Franklin D. Roosevelt was elected president in 1932. By then, the United States had many economic problems. Unemployment was very high. Many people were unable to pay their mortgages or buy enough food. Roosevelt promised people a New Deal. The **New Deal** was a series of federal programs that provided economic help. It cost the U.S. government a great deal of money. But the New Deal led to economic recovery over time.

U.S. History: The 20th Century

The Cold War

After World War II, the alliance between the United States and Soviet Union crumbled. The United States became the leading economic and military power among Western democracies. The Soviet Union sought to extend communism. It wanted to grow its influence in Eastern Europe and parts of Asia. The two nations had very different political systems, economies, and ideals. The competition between these opponents for global power was called the **Cold War.**

Both the United States and Soviet Union controlled powerful nuclear weapons. Their rivalry, therefore, carried the threat of a devastating nuclear war. The two nations never turned the Cold War into an active, or "hot," war. Instead, they gave military and economic aid to other nations that supported their aims. The United States wanted to avoid the expansion of communism at almost any cost. The Korean War and the Vietnam War both took place during the Cold War. Both wars saw a communist power and an anti-communist power struggle for control of a nation.

Rights Movements

African Americans had long experienced racial discrimination. Individuals and groups like the National Association for the Advancement of Colored People (NAACP) had worked against this problem since the early 1900s. Progress was slow, however. In the 1950s, more people began to call for an end to discriminatory laws and practices. These people formed the **Civil Rights Movement**. This movement helped persuade federal lawmakers to pass strong new civil rights laws. These laws made segregation illegal and strengthened protections for African American voters.

The spirit of the Civil Rights Movement encouraged other groups to act. The **feminist** (women's rights) movement made gains in the 1960s and 1970s. Women gained federal protections against employment discrimination. U.S. Supreme Court rulings gave women more control over reproduction. Some women's groups tried to win a constitutional amendment guaranteeing gender equality. But lawmakers failed to ratify the Equal Rights Amendment.

UNIT 2 / LESSON 11

U.S. History: The 20th Century

Interpreting Sources: Muckrakers

The **Progressive Era** began in about 1900 and lasted until World War I. Progressives were reformers. They worked to fix some of the problems caused by industrialization and urbanization. They did this in part by drawing public attention to conditions for working class immigrants and other city dwellers. Journalists called **muckrakers** highlighted social ills in their published works.

Muckrakers wrote books, published articles, and took photographs. Photographer Jacob Riis created a famous series of photos called *How the Other Half Lives*. He showed the problems of immigrants and the working class in New York City. Riis used techniques that journalists avoid today. He posed people for his photos and had them re-enact events. The photos do show life for a group of people, but they are not reliable as an exact record of events in the past.

This is the photographer's hat. Historians think he added it to the scene to suggest a religious halo above the mother's head. Contemporary viewers of the photo would have been familiar with this religious symbolism.

This photograph is called "Italian Mother and Baby." Photographer Jacob Riis probably posed the woman and her child in this way. Their placement at the center of the photo draws the viewer's attention to the woman and her facial expression.

Riis's photos are an important resource for historians to understand the life of the poor in the late 1800s and early 1900s. Think about what you know about the reliability of sources. Do you consider these photos reliable? How can you tell?

Lesson Practice — UNIT 2 / LESSON 11

Complete the activities below to check your understanding of the lesson content.

Vocabulary

Write definitions in your own words for each of the key terms.

1. feminism _____

   _____

2. isolationism _____

   _____

3. militarism _____

   _____

4. muckraker _____

   _____

5. New Deal _____

   _____

6. Treaty of Versailles _____

   _____

UNIT 2 / LESSON 11

Lesson Practice

TEST STRATEGY

Check whether each answer choice is true or false to help you answer multiple choice items. Try out this strategy on Question 9. You can eliminate Choice A because it is false. This means it cannot have been a cause of World War II. Now, decide whether each of the remaining answer choices is true or false.

Apply Your Knowledge

Choose the correct answer to each question.

7. Which of these was a cause of the Great Depression?
   - A   high unemployment
   - B   stock speculation
   - C   federal relief programs
   - D   rise of dictators

8. Which nation was the main U.S. rival in the Cold War?
   - A   Germany
   - B   Italy
   - C   Mexico
   - D   Soviet Union

9. How did the Treaty of Versailles contribute to the start of World War II?
   - A   It did not officially end World War I.
   - B   It contributed to the Great Depression in the United States.
   - C   It encouraged the rise of dictators in Germany and Italy.
   - D   It made European nations give up the policy of isolationism.

10. How did the Civil Rights Movement mostly relate to the rise of the feminist movement?
    - A   Civil rights successes inspired women's rights activists.
    - B   Focus on civil rights slowed progress in women's rights.
    - C   Civil rights and feminist leaders were often the same people.
    - D   Supporters of the feminist movement usually opposed civil rights.

Lesson Practice

UNIT 2 / LESSON 11

Skills Practice

Review the list of sources. Then respond to the questions that follow.

Sources About the Civil Rights Movement

Source A: Blog post by a high school student about civil rights leaders
Source B: Newspaper article about passage of a civil rights law
Source C: Transcription of a speech by a civil rights leader
Source D: Photograph of a civil rights rally
Source E: Encyclopedia article about events in the 1950s and 1960s
Source F: Opinion piece about the civil rights movement

11. Identify three reliable sources from the list.

    _____
    _____

12. Identify two unreliable sources from the list.

    _____
    _____

13. What is one question to help you determine whether each source is unreliable or unreliable?

    _____
    _____

14. Should a historian use an unreliable source in her research? Explain your answer.

    _____
    _____
    _____

See page 92 for answers and help.

> **KEY POINT!**
>
> The 20th century was a time of great conflict and change.

U.S. History: The Modern World

KEY WORDS

- Persian Gulf War
- War on Terror

Change and Conflict

The Soviet Union fell in the early 1990s. Nations in Eastern Europe that had been under Soviet influence began to rebuild. The United States contributed troops to help end conflicts in some of these former communist regions. It also intervened in the Middle East. The **Persian Gulf War** was fought in 1990 and 1991. U.S. troops pushed back an Iraqi invasion of neighboring Kuwait.

The economy grew for much of the 1990s and 2000s. But it suffered a huge setback in the late 2000s. A deep recession raised unemployment and led to calls for reforms of banking practices. Improved communications and transportation made the economy more globalized. China emerged as one of the world's biggest economies. It overtook the United States in terms of total value of goods and services produced in 2014.

In 2001, terrorists made devastating attacks on U.S. soil. They hijacked four commercial airplanes. Terrorist pilots flew two planes into the World Trade Center, which then included the two tallest structures in the United States and was a symbol of its economy. They flew a third plane into the Pentagon, which houses the U.S. military's headquarters. The final plane crashed in a field in Pennsylvania. People believe it was also intended for an attack on Washington, D.C.

The attacks led U.S. leaders to launch a global **War on Terror**. President George W. Bush announced a national strategy to destroy terrorist networks around the world. U.S. troops began fighting in Afghanistan. That nation's government was known to support the terrorist group that had attacked the United States. U.S. leaders also declared war on Iraq. Both wars were long and costly. They became unpopular. Most U.S. troops returned home in the early 2010s, but both regions remained unstable.

U.S. History: The Modern World

UNIT 2 / LESSON 12

Interpreting Sources: Changes in Media Use

People first began to use computers in the mid-1900s. By the 1980s, technology had made computers small enough and cheap enough that some people purchased them for home use. People played games, wrote school papers, or created graphics and visuals. Internet access was very uncommon until the early 1990s. People then began to use their telephone lines to dial in to the World Wide Web. The Internet's offerings were relatively limited. People sent e-mails, talked in chat rooms, or visited simple websites. Faster connection speeds gradually allowed more content to be available on the Internet. This drew more interest. By 2013, nearly three-quarters of U.S. households were using the Internet.

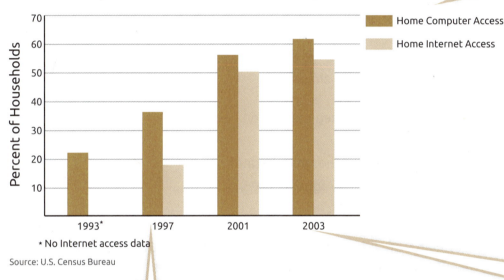

Home Computer and Internet Access, 1993–2003

* No Internet access data
Source: U.S. Census Bureau

Read the title and labels closely. This graph shows the changing levels of home computer ownership and Internet access. It does not include people who used computers only at work or had Internet access at school.

Between 1997 and 2001, computer ownership grew by about 20 percent. At the same time, home Internet access increased by more than 30 percent. You can infer that people who already had computers began gaining access to the Internet. Internet access probably became easier and cheaper during this time.

Consider the huge jump in home Internet usage between 1993 and 2003. It's likely that more people gained home Internet access after the time shown on this graph. What other predictions can you make about the role of the Internet in U.S. society?

UNIT 2 / LESSON 12

Lesson Practice

TEST STRATEGY

When a question asks for the *most likely* response, consider how probable each answer choice is. Use common sense and your own knowledge of a topic to make this determination. Read Question 4. How probable is it that every American will own a smartphone in 2017, as Choice A suggests? This is very unlikely. You can eliminate this choice. Consider the probability of each of the other choices to pick the best answer.

Complete the activities below to check your understanding of the lesson content.

Apply Your Knowledge

Choose the correct answer to each question.

1. Which nation became the biggest U.S. economic competitor by the 2010s?
   A   China
   B   Iraq
   C   Kuwait
   D   Soviet Union

2. What was one main effect of the recession that began in 2008?
   A   The Iraq War began.
   B   Internet access increased.
   C   Stock prices went up.
   D   Unemployment rose sharply.

3. What event directly caused the War on Terror?
   A   Iraq invaded Kuwait.
   B   Terrorists attacked the United States.
   C   U.S. troops invaded Afghanistan.
   D   The Soviet Union fell.

4. In 2011, 35% of all Americans had a smartphone. In 2014, 64% did. What prediction about smartphone ownership in the future is most likely accurate?
   A   Smartphone ownership will reach 100% by 2017.
   B   Smartphone ownership will continue to grow over time.
   C   Smartphone ownership will stay about the same for several years.
   D   Smartphone ownership will quickly decline by 2017.

Lesson Practice

UNIT 2 / LESSON 12

Skills Practice

Read the passage. Then place the events on the timeline in the correct order.

The election of 2000 was closely fought. President Bill Clinton had generated a great deal of controversy during his time in office. But he had won election to two terms, and enjoyed high approval ratings despite these problems. His vice-president, Al Gore, received the Democratic nomination for president. The governor of Texas, George W. Bush, received the Republican nomination. Bush's father had been president during the late 1980s and early 1990s. Clinton defeated the older Bush for president in 1992.

Voters narrowly preferred Gore in the 2000 election. But the president is chosen by special voters in the Electoral College. States usually direct all of their Electoral College representatives to vote for the candidate who wins the vote in the state. This means that the nationwide popular vote and electoral vote do not necessarily match up. The popular vote in Florida was very close. The state did not immediately assign its Electoral College votes, so the election was not decided for weeks. Bush ultimately won Florida, and the election. He became president in January of 2001.

KEY POINT!

The United States underwent a time of great change in the 1990s and 2000s. Technology and international politics made the world more closely interconnected.

5. Add these events to the timeline in the correct sequence:

   Gore becomes the Democratic candidate

   Clinton defeats Bush for president

   George W. Bush becomes president

   Florida's votes are unassigned

See page 93 for answers and help.

Lesson 12 / U.S. History: The Modern World

UNIT 2 — Unit Test

Answer the questions based on the content covered in this unit.

Read the following passage. Then use the passage to answer questions 1 and 2.

> Human civilizations developed independently in at least seven places around Earth. Early people were at first hunter-gatherers. Over time, they learned to grow crops and herd animals. They formed settled societies. These early communities grew as food surpluses increased. Surpluses meant that some people were freed from spending all of their time growing food. People became priests, rulers, and traders.

1. Which of the following led most directly to the development of settled human societies?
   - A domestication of plants and animals
   - B construction of temples and pyramids
   - C development of long-distance trade networks
   - D formation of governments headed by kings

2. How do historians most likely know that long-ago human civilizations developed independently?
   - A due to written records
   - B through archeological research
   - C because of cultural diffusion
   - D from study of maps and charts

Read the following passage. Then, use the passage to answer questions 3–5.

> Born in 356 BCE, Alexander the Great was the son of another Macedonian conqueror, Philip. Philip united the Greek peninsula under Macedonian rule during his reign. Alexander inherited this empire upon his father's death in 336. Quickly, Alexander began a period of great expansion. He led an army of thousands of soldiers into Persia. Persia was a powerful empire to the east. Over the next few years, these forces conquered huge areas of Persian land. By late 332, Alexander had conquered Persian territory across western Asia. He then marched southward toward Egypt. The Egyptians quickly surrendered. Alexander founded a new capital, Alexandria, in northern Egypt.
>
> Alexander then controlled the eastern Mediterranean region. He turned back toward Asia to complete his conquest of Persia. The death of the Persian emperor in 330 made this process easier. Alexander's armies swept across Asia. He captured land in what is now Afghanistan and Uzbekistan. He attempted to move into India in the mid-320s but found the terrain too difficult to overcome.
>
> Alexander the Great died in 323, but his empire lived on. Some of his top generals divided the lands among themselves. They established three Hellenistic kingdoms. Perhaps more importantly, Alexander spread Greek practices across much of the world. He founded cities and spread Greek culture far and wide.

3. Which was most likely a result of Alexander the Great's conquests?
   - A Egypt became the most powerful empire in the West.
   - B Athens and Sparta fought off Persian attacks.
   - C Greek philosophy influenced thinkers in Persia and Central Asia.
   - D Macedonia united all of the Mediterranean into one empire.

4. Based on this passage, which evaluation of Alexander the Great is best supported?
   A   He was a skilled general and tactician.
   B   He was most important for his spread of learning.
   C   He was a less effective monarch than his father.
   D   He treated the people he conquered with unnecessary cruelty.

5. Which territory was conquered by Alexander the Great during the period 332–330 BCE?
   A   Macedonia
   B   Greece
   C   India
   D   Egypt

Consider the following statement.

The Renaissance was the greatest flowering of human achievement in world history.

6. This statement is best classified as
   A   a fact.
   B   an inference.
   C   a bias.
   D   an opinion.

7. Which of the following would be the most reliable source for the study of the development of European imperialism?
   A   a blog post by a high school history teacher, titled "What Caused the Spanish-American War?"
   B   a historical article by a professor, called "Influence of Europe in Africa, 1800–1900"
   C   a student research paper, called "How Christopher Columbus Changed the Americas"
   D   a section of an encyclopedia article, called "Effects of the Triangular Trade, 1500–1700"

8. Three of the following are secondary sources on World War II. Which is a primary source?
   A   documentary film about U.S. involvement in the war
   B   biography of Adolf Hitler written by a German historian
   C   interview with a survivor of the atomic bomb attack on Hiroshima
   D   website showing photos from an Italian museum exhibit

UNIT 2 | Unit Test

Questions 9–11 refer to the map below.

European Exploration of North America, 1500s–1600s

9. Which explorer mostly followed the Mississippi River?
   A La Salle
   B De Soto
   C Cortes
   D Champlain

10. Which is the most likely reason few explorers reached as far as west as did Coronado?
    A They had little interest in the arid region.
    B They were blocked by a strong empire.
    C They were unaware of western lands.
    D They entered the continent from the east.

11. Based on this map, which prediction about European colonies in the 1700s is best supported?
    A Most would be located in the eastern half of North America.
    B They would be very densely populated.
    C Colonies would probably be set up mostly by the Spanish and Portuguese.
    D European countries would likely have little contact with their colonies.

Read the following passage. Then, use the passage to answer questions 12 and 13.

> We the People of the United States, in Order to form a more perfect Union, establish Justice, insure domestic Tranquility, provide for the common defence, promote the general Welfare, and secure the Blessings of Liberty to ourselves and our Posterity, do ordain and establish this Constitution for the United States of America.

12. What problem was this text mostly created to solve?
    A American colonists wished to end rule by the British king.
    B The Articles of Confederation did not form an effective government.
    C U.S. states could not agree how to settle the question of slavery.
    D People worried that the plan for government did not protect individual rights.

13. Who served as the first president under the plan for government given here?
    A James Madison
    B John Adams
    C Thomas Jefferson
    D George Washington

Questions 14 and 15 refer to the following timeline.

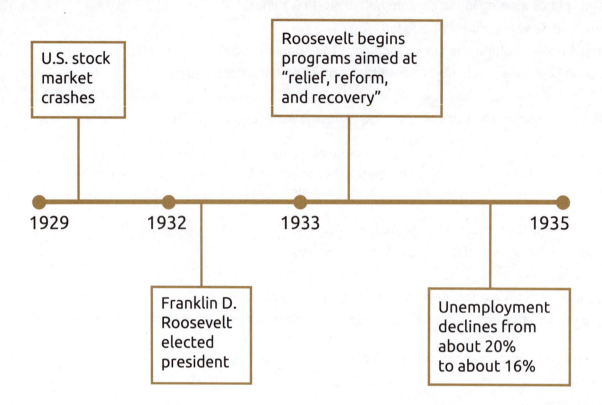

14. Which is the best title for this timeline?
   A Steps toward Isolationism
   B Progressive Era Reforms
   C Causes of World War II
   D Great Depression and New Deal

15. Based on this timeline, what inference about the early 1930s can be made?
   A Interest in political matters was low.
   B Many people were buying and selling stocks.
   C Roosevelt had a low approval rating.
   D Unemployment was higher than 20%.

See page 93 for answers.

Unit Answer Key   UNIT 2

Lesson 1
1. C. Read the Key Point.
2. B. Look for text evidence to directly support the correct answer. Review sentences 4, 5, and 6 to find the answer.
3. A.
4. B. See the Test Strategy for more help on this item.

Lesson 2
1. B. The text says, "Christianity became popular in the Roman Empire." Then it goes on to describe the spread of Christianity.
2. A. See the Test Strategy for more help on this item.
3. D.
4. A. Jesus was a Jew.

Lesson 3
1. D. Nixon does not directly address his feelings about the war. The text does not mention the reasons for the war or when it began.
2. B. See the Test Strategy for more help on this item.

Lesson 4
1. D. No one shall be imprisoned "… except by the lawful judgment of his equals."
2. C. See the Test Strategy for more help on this item.
3. Correct order: Leonardo da Vinci trains as a painter; Leonardo da Vinci paints *The Last Supper*; Leonardo da Vinci makes scientific observations; The *Mona Lisa* is displayed in Paris

Lesson 5
1. the use of power by one country to rule another
2. the making of goods in factories
3. theory in which colonies exist to supply raw materials to and buy finished goods from their ruling countries
4. route from Africa to the Americas carrying millions of enslaved people as ship cargo
5. a set of routes connecting the Americas, Europe, and West Africa

   One way to remember this meaning is to imagine the triangle between these regions on a map.
6. growth of cities
7. A. Look for the line with the highest point. The line for Brazil reaches about 850,000 in the 1700s.
8. C. Look at the dates on the graph. Europeans were just beginning to explore and settle in the Americas.
9. C. See the Test Strategy for more help on this item.

Lesson 6
1. B. Read the first sentence—main idea—of each paragraph.
2. A. See the Test Strategy for more help on this item.
3. Source X is more reliable. It was written by an expert and gives facts and information without much bias. Source Y is a blog post. It does not cite sources and contains more opinion than facts.

Lesson 7
1. D. One of the answer choices can be eliminated easily—scientists, because you might realize that the age of science did not occur until thousands of years after the earliest settlers came to the Americas.
2. A. Think about what problem irrigation solved.
3. B.
4. C. See the Test Strategy for more help on this item.
5. Cold temperatures froze water to create a land bridge.
6. They were able to practice agriculture.
7. They built a road network.

Lesson 8
1. A. Think about the word *conquistador*. It sounds like "conquest."
2. D. The Spanish settled in St. Augustine in 1565.
3. D. See the Test Strategy for more help on this item.
4. C. All of these statements give facts. To answer this question, think about which fact most tells why New England had little slavery.
5. Sample answer: Both had economies based on agriculture.
6. Sample answer: New England did not have good land for farming.
7. Sample answer: The Middle Colonies and Southern Colonies were most alike. They both relied on agriculture for farming and were located next to each other.

Lesson 9
1. refusal to buy something
2. plan for government
3. support for one's own nation
4. British policy limiting western colonization
5. B. See the Test Strategy for more help on this item.
6. A. If it is difficult to identify examples of nationalism, you can try eliminating answer choices that do not fit the time period of the early 1800s. If you recall that the U.S. Constitution was written in the 1700s, you can easily eliminate answer B.

Unit 2 / History

91

UNIT 2 — Unit Answer Key

7. B. Under the Articles of Confederation, the Northwest Ordinances were passed to organize the western territories.

8. Sample answer: The Proclamation of 1763 limited western settlement, but the Northwest Ordinances encouraged it. This was a change.

9. Sample answer: Both of these documents organized the national government. They were important to running the United States. This was a continuity.

10. Sample answer: The French and Indian War spread British land claims. It made Britain stronger in the Americas. But it also led to colonial anger. This in turn contributed to the American Revolution. Today, the United States exists in part because of the effects of this war.

Lesson 10

1. Fugitive Slave Law
2. Kansas-Nebraska Act
3. secede Consider whether the answer choices fit the question grammatically. Secede and abolish are the only two verbs in the answer bank, so those answers only fit questions 3 and 5.
4. popular sovereignty
5. abolish
6. Manifest Destiny
7. sectionalism
8. segregation
9. C. See the Test Strategy for more help on this item.
10. A. The Missouri Compromise admitted Missouri and Maine—one free state and one slave state.
11. D. Manifest Destiny was the idea that the U.S. should stretch all the way west toward the Pacific Ocean.
12. C. Southern states continued to deny rights to African Americans.

13. B. Use the word *most* in the question to quickly figure out the answer. Urban factories were in cities with large populations, so that is a clue that indicates the correct answer.

14. This illustration shows white Southerners and freed slaves.

15. Sample answer: These groups likely disagreed on how former slaves should be treated. They probably also disagreed about how much influence the North should have in the South.

16. Sample answer: I think the illustrator did not think it was a success. The two groups are shown as angry and willing to fight each other. Only the figure in the center keeps them from starting a new war. Some photos or illustrations will include text or signs that give you clear clues about what is going on. Since there is no text in this illustration, you must interpret the meaning in other ways. Look at the people's gestures and expressions. Notice that they are carrying weapons and are waving them, apparently in anger. Also note that the illustrator has shown the two groups facing each other in opposition. These clues tell you that the illustrator probably does not think Reconstruction was a success.

17. Sample answer: A former Confederate would probably have been angry. The illustration shows white Southerners as angry and disorganized. They still want to fight. It does not show them in a very positive way.

Lesson 11

1. support for women's rights

    One way of studying and remembering the meanings of key words is to think about the words' roots. The root of *feminism* is *fem*, which you probably relate to *female*, or woman. This is a clue that *feminism* relates to women's rights.

2. policy in favor of staying neutral

3. focus on the building up of a nation's military
4. journalist who worked during the Progressive Era
5. federal programs to combat the Great Depression
6. treaty ending World War I
7. B. When a question asks you to identify *causes*, you can possibly eliminate answer choices that are actually *effects*. Thinking about it this way, you might remember that choices A and C were actually effects of the Great Depression, not causes.
8. D.
9. C. See the Test Strategy for more help on this item.
10. A.
11. Any three of the following: Source B, Source C, Source D, and Source E

    Opinion writing cannot be used as reliable sources because the author may not present all relevant facts. Blogs cannot be trusted as reliable sources because it is not always possible to make sure the author is an expert on the subject matter. The other sources on the list have been published by trusted companies, so they are usually reliable.

12. Source A and Source F
13. Sample answer: Does this source accurately reflect real people, places, and events?
14. Sample answer: A historian could use some kinds of unreliable sources in her research as long as she understood that they had problems. Unreliable sources show what some people think or believe about a topic. They might also contain some elements of truth. Jacob Riis's photos, for example, can be considered unreliable because he posed them. But they still show real people and places.

Unit Answer Key — UNIT 2

Lesson 12

1. A. As the U.S. fell into a deep recession, China's economy continued to grow.
2. D. During a recession, the economy is declining or depressed. Unemployment is a direct result of a decline in the economy.
3. B. The terrorist attacks on the U.S. on September 11, 2001, caused the War on Terror.
4. B. See the Test Strategy for more help on this item.
5. Correct sequence: Clinton defeats Bush for president; Gore becomes the Democratic candidate; Florida's votes are unassigned; George W. Bush becomes president

Unit Test

1. A.
2. B.
3. C.
4. A.
5. D.
6. D.
7. B.
8. C.
9. A.
10. D.
11. A.
12. B.
13. D.
14. D.
15. D.

Unit Glossary

- **abolish** — end forever
- **agriculture** — farming
- **Articles of Confederation** — first governing document of the United States that gave most power to the states
- **atomic bomb** — powerful military weapon using nuclear technology
- **bias** — personal opinion that shapes how someone views a topic
- **boycott** — refuse to buy
- **Byzantine Empire** — empire based at Constantinople that was once part of the Roman Empire
- **caravel** — light, mobile Portuguese ship
- **cash crop** — crop grown to sell for a profit
- **city-state** — independent city with its own government and citizenship
- **Civil Rights Movement** — period of people working together to end legalized racial discrimination
- **Cold War** — competition between the United States and Soviet Union for global power
- **Compromise of 1850** — agreement that admitted California and made new rules about the possible expansion of slavery westward
- **conquistadors** — Spanish adventures and conquerors during the Age of Exploration
- **constitution** — plan for government
- **Continental Congress** — meeting of colonial leaders
- **cuneiform** — ancient writing cut into clay tablets
- **Dark Ages** — time period from about 500 to 1000 with little surviving recorded history
- **Declaration of Independence** — document announcing American independence from Great Britain
- **democracy** — political system in which citizens vote directly on leaders and laws
- **dynasty** — ruling families in which the kingship passes from generation to generation
- **Equal Rights Amendment** — proposed constitutional amendment guaranteeing gender equality
- **fact** — statement that can be proven true
- **feminism** — women's rights
- **Fugitive Slave Law** — controversial law that required all U.S. citizens to help capture and return runaway slaves to their owners
- **Great Depression** — period of worldwide economic downtown during the 1930s
- **hieroglyphics** — writing that uses pictures to show ideas or syllables
- **Homestead Act** — law of 1862 giving people free land in the West under certain conditions
- **hunter-gatherer** — people who survive by collecting wild plants and hunting
- **imperialism** — use of power by one country to rule another
- **industrialization** — making of goods in factories
- **irrigation** — systems to move water for farming
- **isolationism** — policy of staying out of global conflicts
- **Kansas-Nebraska Act** — law overturning the Missouri Compromise and allowing people in Kansas and Nebraska to vote on whether to allow slavery

Unit Glossary — UNIT 2

- **labor specialization** — division of labor in which people do different jobs
- **Manifest Destiny** — idea that the United States had a duty to expand to the Pacific Ocean
- **mercantilism** — theory stating that colonies existed to provide raw materials and markets for their ruling country
- **Mesoamerica** — region of Mexico, Central America, and South America settled by people long ago
- **Middle Passage** — long, difficult Atlantic crossing that was part of the slave trade
- **militarism** — national focus on building military power
- **Missouri Compromise** — agreement of 1820 that admitted Missouri and Maine, and tried to end debate over slavery
- **muckraker** — journalists who wrote about social problems
- **nationalism** — support for one's own nation above others
- **Native Americans** — native group of what is now the United States
- **New Deal** — series of federal programs that provided economic help during the Great Depression
- **opinion** — statement that gives a person's idea about a topic
- **Persian Gulf War** — war fought in and around Iraq in 1990 and 1991
- **popular sovereignty** — voting by the people
- **primary source** — source created by someone who witnessed an event
- **Proclamation of 1763** — British policy setting a western limit for colonial settlement
- **Progressive Era** — period of social, political, and economic reform lasting between about 1900 and 1915
- **Reformation** — European religious reform movement
- **Renaissance** — period of cultural flowering and rebirth in Europe
- **republic** — political system in which citizens vote for leaders who then make laws on their behalf
- **secede** — formally leave a country
- **secondary source** — source created by someone about an event that he or she did not witness
- **sectionalism** — support for one's own region rather than the whole nation
- **segregation** — legal separation of people by race
- **self-government** — overseeing of a community's political affairs by its own representatives
- **speculation** — buying something with the intention of selling it later at a profit
- **Transcontinental Railroad** — long-distance railroad linking the Atlantic and Pacific Oceans
- **Treaty of Versailles** — agreement ending World War I that punished Germany for the war
- **triangular trade** — set of routes connecting the Americas, Europe, and West Africa over which raw materials, finished goods, and enslaved humans traveled
- **urbanization** — growth of cities
- **War on Terror** — U.S. strategy to destroy terrorist networks around the world

Study More!

World History: Pre-History and the Ancient World
- Neanderthals
- Cave paintings
- Pyramids, ziggurats, and other monumental architecture
- Development of the alphabet
- Fertile Crescent and Indus River Valley civilizations
- Development of religions including Judaism and Hinduism

World History: Classical Civilizations
- Persian Wars
- Pax Romana
- Decline of the Roman Empire
- Silk Roads and long-distance trade
- Development of religions and philosophies including Christianity, Buddhism, and Confucianism

Skills: Fact and Opinion
- Bias

World History: The Early Modern Period
- The Crusades
- Viking explorations
- Urban growth
- Trade leagues
- Islamic conquest and expansion
- Development of religions including Islam

World History: A Globalized World
- The Enlightenment and Enlightened monarchs
- French Revolution
- Opening of Japan and the Meiji restoration
- Karl Marx and the development of communism
- The Russian Revolution

Skills: Reliability of Sources
- Propaganda

U.S. History: Pre-Columbian Americas
- Native American nations
- Inca labor
- Mesoamerican religious beliefs and practices

U.S. History: Colonization and Settlement
- Pilgrims and Puritans
- Quakers
- Royal and charter colonies
- Virginia Company

U.S. History: The Early Republic
- Boston Tea Party
- Loyalists
- Louisiana Purchase
- Rise of political parties
- Administrations of Washington, Adams, and Jefferson
- War of 1812
- Invention of the cotton gin

Study More! — UNIT 2

U.S. History: Civil War and Industrialization
- Abolitionism
- Dred Scott decision
- Election of 1860
- Ulysses S. Grant and Robert E. Lee
- Civil War shortages
- Wagon trails
- Chinese immigration
- Inventors and inventions

U.S. History: The 20th Century
- Women's suffrage
- Roaring Twenties
- First and Second Red Scare
- Vietnam War
- Watergate
- Space race and arms race
- End of the Cold War

U.S. History: The Modern World
- Impeachment of Bill Clinton
- Bush v. Gore
- North American Free Trade Agreement (NAFTA)
- al-Qaeda and ISIS

UNIT 3

Civics & Government

Do you have a driving license? In order to receive a license, you had to follow a number of steps. You probably applied at a state agency for a permit to learn to drive. You probably had to follow certain rules and laws, like driving only with a fully licensed driver in the vehicle. After you felt confident in your skills, you took a test. When you passed the test, the state issued you a license—an exciting day! The government managed all of these steps. Activities like these make government a part of people's everyday lives. About one-third of all the social studies items on the HiSET® will ask you to use your knowledge of the U.S. government, politics, and civic participation.

KEY WORDS

- Articles of Confederation
- bicameral legislature
- bill
- Bill of Rights
- Cabinet
- campaign
- candidate
- charter
- checks and balances
- citizen
- conclusion
- Congress
- Constitution
- council-manager system
- court-packing plan
- Democratic Party
- Electoral College
- executive branch
- executive privilege
- federalism
- functional document
- general election
- government
- governor
- House of Representatives
- immigrant
- inference
- judicial activism
- judicial branch
- judicial review
- Judiciary Act of 1789
- legislative branch
- lobbyist
- mayor-council system
- municipal government
- naturalization
- platform
- political action committee (PAC)
- political party
- precedent
- primary election
- Republican Party
- Senate
- Speaker of the House
- special interest group
- super PAC
- voter registration form

Forms of Government

UNIT 3 / LESSON 1

KEY WORDS
- federalism
- government

Organizing Government

Government is any system people use to manage a country, region, or community. Governments make and enforce laws for citizens to follow. Often, they collect money from citizens to be used for shared resources, like roads or public safety.

Review the table below to learn about some common forms of government over time.

Type of Government	Main Ruler and Decision Maker
Absolute monarchy	Hereditary king or queen
Communist state	Leader or leaders of the communist party
Democracy	Citizens
Dictatorship	One unelected ruler
Military junta	Group of military leaders
Parliamentary monarchy	Elected legislature; some input by hereditary king or queen
Republic	Elected representatives; some input by president or other elected head
Theocracy	Religious leader or leaders

The characteristics of forms of government can overlap; absolute monarchies and dictatorships, for example, are both led by unelected rulers.

In the United States, citizens vote in elections for leaders. These leaders, in turn, make, enforce, and interpret laws and policies for all citizens. This means that the United States is a republic. Government power is shared between the national government and smaller independent units called states. This division of power creates a system called **federalism**.

UNIT 3 / LESSON 1

Lesson Practice

KEY POINT!

Common democratic forms of government in the world today include republics and constitutional monarchies.

TEST STRATEGY

Look for evidence in the text to help you answer questions based on reading passages. Read Question 4 carefully. Find the section of the reading passage that tells a major change in Europe. The fall of the Roman Empire was a turning point in how European governments worked.

Complete the activities below to check your understanding of the lesson content.

Skills Practice

Read the text. Then choose the correct answer to each question.

For many centuries, the Roman Empire firmly controlled Western Europe. The Empire had a strong centralized government with political power coming from the emperor. Appointed governors and officials exercised power over smaller regions on behalf of the emperor. After the Roman Empire fell, no single strong power replaced it. European monarchs officially ruled countries. In practice, however, they often lacked power over their lands. Lords of the aristocracy, or landed elite, oversaw the real management of their territories.

1. According to the passage, which of these people was a member of the aristocracy?
   A a lord who owned a great deal of farmland
   B a European king who officially controlled a nation
   C a provincial governor given his job by the emperor
   D a government official who managed Roman affairs

2. The Roman Empire is best characterized as what form of government?
   A constitutional monarchy
   B dictatorship
   C republic
   D theocracy

3. Based on the information in the passage, what was one similarity between the Roman emperor and later European kings?
   A Both ruled over strong central governments.
   B Both officially held a great deal of political power.
   C Both struggled to maintain control over the aristocracy.
   D Both opposed the rise of democratic governments.

4. Based on the passage, what was the main cause of the shifts in government power in medieval Europe?
   A Governors oversaw Roman provinces.
   B European monarchs were unelected.
   C Aristocrats controlled large land areas.
   D The Roman Empire fell from power.

See page 143 for answers and help.

U.S. Founding Documents

UNIT 3 / LESSON 2

Establishing U.S. Government

The U.S. founding documents are the texts that establish the nation's system of government and state its basic political ideals. During colonial times, **charters** issued by monarchs or by companies like the Virginia Company were common founding documents. These gave colonists the right to settle on lands claimed by European powers. The Mayflower Compact was another colonial founding document. It said that the Pilgrims agreed to form a group for the purposes of self-government.

The Declaration of Independence was written in 1776. It laid out Americans' reasons for rejecting the rule of the British king. This document stated key democratic principles that influenced how Americans set up their government and laws. The first U.S. government was organized under the **Articles of Confederation**. The Articles strictly limited the power of the national government. Leaders decided to revise the Articles only a few years after they were adopted. They replaced them with a new plan for government, the U.S. **Constitution**.

Many U.S. leaders were uncertain about the Constitution. They worried it gave the government too much power at the expense of citizens and states. Supporters of the Constitution were called Federalists. Three Federalists wrote a series of essays intended to explain the Constitution's ideals and to encourage people to support its adoption. These essays, known as the Federalist Papers, are an important historical source of information about the thinking behind the Constitution. U.S. leaders decided to add a **Bill of Rights** to the Constitution to protect individual liberties. They looked to an earlier English Bill of Rights for inspiration. The addition of the Bill of Rights helped secure adoption of the U.S. Constitution in 1789.

KEY WORDS

- Articles of Confederation
- Bill of Rights
- charter
- checks and balances
- Constitution
- executive branch
- judicial branch
- legislative branch

U.S. Founding Documents

Interpreting Sources: U.S. Constitution

The Constitution was written in 1787 and is still used today. This document sets up the framework for U.S. federal government. It establishes three branches of government. The **legislative branch** makes laws. The **judicial branch** interprets laws. The **executive branch** enforces laws. Each of these branches has the constitutional authority to limit the power of the other branches in some way. This creates a system of **checks and balances**, which keeps any one branch from becoming too powerful.

> We the People of the United States, in Order to form a more perfect Union, establish Justice, insure domestic Tranquility, provide for the common defence, promote the general Welfare, and secure the Blessings of Liberty to ourselves and our Posterity, do ordain and establish this Constitution for the United States of America....

The opening paragraph of the Constitution is known as the Preamble. The Preamble states the purpose of the Constitution and gives some of its ideals, such as liberty.

Article I, Section 1.

All legislative Powers herein granted shall be vested in a Congress of the United States, which shall consist of a Senate and House of Representatives....

Article II, Section 1.

The executive Power shall be vested in a President of the United States of America. He shall hold his Office during the Term of four Years, and, together with the Vice President, chosen for the same Term, be elected, as follows....

Article III, Section 1.

The judicial Power of the United States, shall be vested in one supreme Court, and in such inferior Courts as the Congress may from time to time ordain and establish....

The Constitution is organized into Articles and Sections. Each of these deals with a different aspect of setting up and running the government. These Articles create and explain each branch of government.

Article V.

The Congress, whenever two thirds of both Houses shall deem it necessary, shall propose Amendments to this Constitution, or, on the Application of the Legislatures of two thirds of the several States, shall call a Convention for proposing Amendments, which .. shall be valid ... as Part of this Constitution, when ratified by the Legislatures of three fourths of the several States, or by Conventions in three fourths thereof ...

Article V gives a series of steps through which the Constitution may be amended, or changed. The Constitution has been amended 27 times.

Lesson Practice

UNIT 3 / LESSON 2

Complete the activities below to check your understanding of the lesson content.

Apply Your Knowledge

Complete the table. First, categorize each document into correct time period by adding the words colonial era, American Revolution, or Early Republic to the first column. Then, write a short description of each document in the second column.

Founding Document	Era	Description
1. Mayflower Compact		
2. Declaration of Independence		
3. Articles of Confederation		
4. Federalist Papers		

KEY POINT!

The U.S. government and its ideals were created by several written documents, especially the U.S. Constitution.

Lesson 2 / U.S. Founding Documents

103

UNIT 3 / LESSON 2

Lesson Practice

Skills Practice

Read the text. Then choose the correct answer to each question.

Amendment I

Congress shall make no law respecting an establishment of religion, or prohibiting the free exercise thereof; or abridging the freedom of speech, or of the press; or the right of the people peaceably to assemble, and to petition the Government for a redress of grievances....

Amendment IV

The right of the people to be secure in their persons, houses, papers, and effects, against unreasonable searches and seizures, shall not be violated, and no Warrants shall issue, but upon probable cause, supported by Oath or affirmation, and particularly describing the place to be searched, and the persons or things to be seized....

Amendment VII

In Suits at common law, ... the right of trial by jury shall be preserved, and no fact tried by a jury, shall be otherwise re-examined in any Court of the United States, than according to the rules of the common law.

TEST STRATEGY

When a question asks you to identify something that is not true or is least important, use the process of elimination to narrow down your answer choices. Reread Question 7. Now review each answer choice against the text given in the passage. Which of these choices cannot be supported using the text?

5. What historical reason explains the direct reason for the creation of this document?
   - A Disagreements threatened the adoption of the U.S. Constitution.
   - B Americans were unhappy with the rule of the British king.
   - C Weaknesses in the national government worried U.S. leaders.
   - D Colonists wished to establish a system of self-government.

6. The amendments given here relate mostly to
   - A branches of government.
   - B government duties.
   - C checks and balances.
   - D individual liberties.

7. Which right is NOT protected by the Bill of Rights?
   - A the right to practice no religion
   - B the right to work against the government
   - C the right to have a jury trial
   - D the right to refuse unfair searches

See page 143 for answers and help.

Inferences and Conclusions

UNIT 3 / LESSON 3

Making Inferences and Conclusions

An **inference** is an assumption based on facts. It tells something you can figure out based just on the information you have. A **conclusion** uses facts to reach an assumption that goes a step beyond what is known. However, conclusions are also supported closely by facts.

Consider the following two statements. *Thomas Jefferson wrote the Declaration of Independence. The Declaration of Independence was a founding U.S. document.* You can infer that Thomas Jefferson contributed to the ideas of founding U.S. documents. This is strongly suggested just by the facts given by the author. You can also conclude that Thomas Jefferson supported the American Revolution. This is not stated directly by the facts given, but it makes sense based on those facts.

Follow these steps to make inferences and conclusions:

Step 1: Read the text. Note important facts given by the author.

Step 2: To make an inference, ask, *What is strongly suggested by these facts?* Be sure to stick to just the facts that are given.

Step 3: To make a conclusion, ask, *What else must be true based on these facts?* Think about how you can go just one step beyond the facts given.

Inferences and conclusions are similar—sometimes, people even use these words to mean the same thing. You probably won't need to differentiate between inferences and conclusions, but you should know how to recognize them.

KEY WORDS

- conclusion
- inference

UNIT 3 / LESSON 3

Lesson Practice

KEY POINT!

Arrive at inferences and conclusions by determining what is suggested, but not directly stated, by a passage.

TEST STRATEGY

Read the answer choices carefully to determine whether you have enough information to support them. An inference or conclusion that is supported by the text will be clearly suggested. If you are uncertain whether a choice is supported, it is probably a wrong answer. Read Question 2. Do you have enough information to make a determination about choice A?

Complete the activities below to check your understanding of the lesson content.

Skills Practice

Read the text below. Then answer the questions that follow.

The Constitutional Convention approved the new plan for government in the summer of 1787. But the states had to ratify the document for it to go into effect. Some state leaders were reluctant. These people, known as Anti-Federalists, worried the Constitution made the national government too powerful. Supporters of the Constitution were known as Federalists. In the spring and summer of 1788, some supporters published a series of essays called the Federalist papers. These essays sought to convince New York leaders to ratify the Constitution. Although the Federalist papers were written under a pseudonym, historians agree that the authors were James Madison, Alexander Hamilton, and John Jay.

The Federalist papers made strong arguments for the Constitution. The authors claimed that the national government's power rested with the majority, for example. But they also pointed out that it protected people's rights even if those people did not agree with the majority. They believed this encouraged a just government. These and other points helped persuade Anti-Federalists. The new Constitution was adopted in 1789.

1. Based on the passage, what conclusion about the writers of the Federalist Papers is best supported?
   - A They believed a strong central government could respect individual liberties.
   - B They did not have the authority to vote for or against ratification themselves.
   - C They knew their ideas about constitutional principles were a minority view.
   - D They wanted to use their status as political leaders to persuade others to agree with them.

2. Which inference about New York is best supported by the passage?
   - A It was the home of Madison, Hamilton, and Jay.
   - B Its state leaders included many Anti-Federalists.
   - C It had refused to send delegates to the Constitutional Convention.
   - D It ratified the Constitution before the spring of 1789.

See page 143 for answers and help.

The U.S. Congress

UNIT 3 / LESSON 4

Characteristics and Duties of the U.S. Congress

The U.S. Constitution created **Congress** to be the nation's legislative branch. Congress is a **bicameral legislature**, or a lawmaking body with two houses. One house of Congress is the **House of Representatives**. This house currently has 435 members. The number of representatives is determined by each state's population. States like California and Florida with large populations have many representatives, but states like Wyoming and Delaware with small populations have just one. The other house of Congress is the **Senate**. Each state has two senators regardless of its population.

The majority party in the House chooses a leader, known as the **Speaker of the House**. The Speaker has an important role in managing the House's debate over proposed laws. The Speaker also assigns other members of the House to committees and performs other oversight duties. All members of the House, including the Speaker, are elected to two-year terms. The official head of the Senate is the vice president, who is also a member of the executive branch. The vice president normally only takes part in Senate votes in order to break a tie. Members of the Senate are elected to serve for six years.

The legislative branch is mostly responsible for making laws. It also has checks on the other branches, however. Congress must approve some actions and decisions made by the executive branch. For example, Congress has the power to confirm or reject the president's nominees to certain offices. Congress can use this power to exercise influence over the judicial branch since the president appoints justices to the U.S. Supreme Court.

KEY WORDS

- bicameral legislature
- bill
- Congress
- House of Representatives
- Senate
- Speaker of the House

The U.S. Congress

Interpreting Sources: The Legislative Process

Congress's main job is making laws. Every law begins as a proposal called a **bill**. Members of Congress debate and vote on bills. If a bill is approved by Congress, it goes to the president for approval. Many bills never reach this stage, however. A committee can choose to vote down a bill. So can the general membership of each house of Congress. Review the flowchart to see how a bill becomes a law.

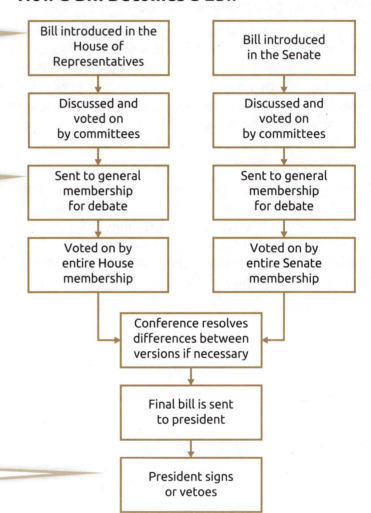

How a Bill Becomes a Law

- Bills can begin in either house of Congress. Ideas for bills come from legislators, special interest groups, the president, or other citizens. → Bill introduced in the House of Representatives

- In the Senate, members can slow debate or attempt to prevent a vote by giving long speeches called filibusters. Senators do this when they know a bill they oppose is likely to pass. → Sent to general membership for debate

- Congress can overturn a president's veto with a two-thirds majority vote. However, this does not happen often. → President signs or vetoes

Flowchart:
1. Bill introduced in the House of Representatives / Bill introduced in the Senate
2. Discussed and voted on by committees
3. Sent to general membership for debate
4. Voted on by entire House membership / Voted on by entire Senate membership
5. Conference resolves differences between versions if necessary
6. Final bill is sent to president
7. President signs or vetoes

Lesson Practice

UNIT 3 / LESSON 4

Complete the activities below to check your understanding of the lesson content.

KEY POINT!

The legislative branch of the United States is Congress. Congress makes laws.

Vocabulary

Write definitions in your own words for each of the key terms.

1. bicameral legislature _____
   _____

2. bill _____
   _____

3. Congress _____
   _____

4. House of Representatives _____
   _____

5. Senate _____
   _____

6. Speaker of the House _____
   _____

Lesson Practice

Skills Practice

Review the graphic organizer. Then choose the correct answer to each question.

Step-By-Step: Bill to Law	
Step	**What Happens?**
1	Bill introduced in House or Senate
2	Committee discusses and studies bill
3	Committee votes on whether to send bill to the floor
4	
5a	Approved bill goes to the other house to repeat process
5b	Rejected bill goes back to committee for revision or is considered dead
6	Bill approved by both houses goes to the president for approval

7. What step should be added to the empty box?
   A   Bill goes to conference to resolve differences
   B   Bill with strong support goes directly to president
   C   Full House or Senate debates and votes on bill
   D   Vetoed bill returns to committee for a new vote

8. Emma is using this chart for a presentation in government class. How can she improve it?
   A   She should add an arrow from Step 1 to Step 6.
   B   She should add an explanation of how Congress checks the president.
   C   She should add a definition of the term *special interest group*.
   D   She should add a step telling what options the president has.

See page 143 for answers and help.

TEST STRATEGY

Study diagrams and graphic aids carefully to ensure you understand their meaning. Pay careful attention to information that seems to be missing or incorrect. You can predict answers to questions like Question 8 by filling in these blanks for yourself as you study a diagram.

The Changing Power of the President

UNIT 3 / LESSON 5

Growth of Executive Power

As the nation's founders set up the government, they wanted to be sure that the United States would never be ruled by a king. The Articles of Confederation had no executive leader. The Constitution, however, created an executive branch headed by a president. The president's constitutional duties were limited. They mostly related to enforcing laws. They included nominating justices to the U.S. Supreme Court, overseeing executive agencies, and approving or vetoing bills passed by Congress. Presidents also have the power to negotiate treaties. They are closely involved with the making of foreign policy.

Over time, individual presidents shaped how the office worked. George Washington was the first president. He set several important **precedents**, or ways of doing things. Washington discouraged U.S. involvement in foreign affairs. He set up the first **Cabinet**. The Cabinet is a group of presidential advisers. He also limited himself to two terms. Other presidents grew the office. Thomas Jefferson used his authority to negotiate treaties to make the Louisiana Purchase. Abraham Lincoln used an executive order to abolish slavery in rebellious states during the Civil War.

As the presidency got stronger, relations between the executive branch and other branches were sometimes tense. During the 1930s, Democratic President Franklin D. Roosevelt spearheaded a broad series of federal programs known as the New Deal. Congress was also controlled by Democrats at this time. It passed Roosevelt's programs and supported his ideas. The U.S. Supreme Court, however, worried that some programs overstepped the constitutional powers of the federal government. They overturned some of Roosevelt's signature programs. Roosevelt then attempted to dramatically reshape the Supreme Court. His plan would have allowed presidents more power to pick judges likely to support their own ideas. This **court-packing plan** proved unpopular. It was rejected. The Supreme Court kept its check on presidential power.

KEY WORDS

- Cabinet
- court-packing plan
- precedent

KEY POINT!

In Article II of the Constitution, the Commander in Chief clause gives the president power over the U.S. army and navy.

The Changing Power of the President

Interpreting Sources: King Andrew

Andrew Jackson was president between 1829 and 1837. He believed in acting decisively as president. For example, Jackson forced South Carolinians to agree to a tax that they disliked. He also challenged the checks and balances written into the Constitution. He refused to abide by a U.S. Supreme Court decision about Native American lands. His strong opinions made him unpopular with some Americans. However, historians generally agree that Jackson transformed the presidency. He made the office into one of stronger leadership and influence than it had been before his time.

The artist uses symbols of monarchy to suggest that Jackson is acting like a king rather than a president. Notice the crown, scepter, and embellished robe.

This cartoon was created shortly after Jackson vetoed a bill that renewed the charter for the Bank of the United States. Jackson then ordered that all federal deposits be removed from the Bank. Some Americans thought Jackson's decision to remove the deposits went beyond his constitutional powers.

Jackson's actions as president pushed the limits of constitutional authority. Here he is shown stepping on the constitution.

Lesson Practice

UNIT 3 / LESSON 5

Complete the activities below to check your understanding of the lesson content.

Apply Your Knowledge

Choose the correct answer to each question.

1. Which of these is the main job of members of the Cabinet?
   A   helping the president get elected
   B   giving the president policy advice
   C   managing relations between the president and Congress
   D   deciding whether a president's actions are constitutional

2. Why did the Articles of Confederation fail to include an executive branch?
   A   The nation was large and had no need for a strong central government.
   B   American politicians could not agree on the right person to head the branch.
   C   The U.S. Constitution had already explained the jobs of the president.
   D   Leaders feared creating a government too much like the British monarchy.

3. Which of these is a main job of the president?
   A   leading the military
   B   electing the vice president
   C   choosing members of Congress
   D   suggesting constitutional amendments

4. Why was Andrew Jackson's refusal to abide by the Supreme Court's decision about Native American lands unconstitutional?
   A   The president lacks any sort of check over the actions of the Supreme Court.
   B   The president does not have the constitutional right to pick Supreme Court justices.
   C   The president does not have the constitutional right to ignore the Supreme Court.
   D   The president lacks the authority to manage federal lands designated by the Supreme Court.

TEST STRATEGY

Use what you already know about a topic to predict answers to some questions. Read Question 2. Cover the answer choices with your hand without reading them. Predict your own answer to the question. Then, take away your hand and review the choices. Which one is closest to your own ideas?

UNIT 3 / LESSON 5

KEY POINT!

The president heads the executive branch. The office of the presidency has become stronger over time.

Lesson Practice

Skills Practice

Review the political cartoon. Then write complete sentences to answer each question that follows.

This political cartoon is from 1832. It shows President Andrew Jackson having a nightmare in which he fights against Congress's approval of the charter for the Bank of the United States. Jackson opposed the Bank.

5. Congress is shown as a monster with many heads. What is the artist suggesting by using this image?

   _____
   _____
   _____

6. Do you think the artist views Jackson in a good way or a negative way? Explain your answer.

   _____
   _____
   _____

See page 143 for answers and help.

Landmark Supreme Court Decisions

Creation of the Judicial Branch

The U.S. Constitution lays out some of the main duties of the judicial branch. Article III establishes the Supreme Court and says that its members are appointed for as long as they wish to serve, so long as they fulfill their jobs faithfully. It also states that the judicial branch has the power to interpret laws and make judgments in certain cases. These include those that relate to the Constitution, national law, or disputes between states. The U.S. government also set up other federal courts to help interpret the nation's laws. The Constitution gives Congress the right to establish these courts.

The Constitution left many details of the court system undefined. Congress filled in these details over time. The **Judiciary Act of 1789** established the U.S. Supreme Court and many lower federal courts. The early Supreme Court had six justices. Over time, the Court expanded. It has been comprised of nine justices since 1869.

The Supreme Court has a strong check on the other branches through the power of **judicial review**. Judicial review is the examination of laws and actions to determine whether they are constitutional. The Court asserted that it had this power in the 1803 decision in *Marbury* v. *Madison*. The Court ruled that part of the Judiciary Act was unconstitutional in this decision. In doing so, it set a precedent for the work of the Court in the years to come.

Although the power of judicial review is not stated in the Constitution, Americans generally accept that this is a job of the U.S. Supreme Court. The practice of **judicial activism** is more controversial. Judicial activism is using the power of the Court to make changes to laws or society. For example, the Court's use of its power of judicial review to end segregation in schools was judicial activism.

KEY WORDS

- executive privilege
- judicial activism
- judicial review
- Judiciary Act of 1789

Landmark Supreme Court Decisions

Selected Landmark Court Decisions

Today, the Supreme Court receives requests to hear some 10,000 cases each year. The Court decides which cases it will consider. It only accepts a very small percentage of these requests. Nevertheless, the Court has heard thousands of cases since it first met in 1790. Some of these cases are considered landmark decisions. This is because they set important legal precedents or changed the way governments and citizens interacted. Review the following table to learn about some landmark decisions. Notice that some of these, such as the *Dred Scott* decision, have been overturned by later constitutional changes or Court opinions.

Landmark Supreme Court Decisions		
Case	Year Decided	Outcome
McCulloch v. Maryland	1819	Congress had the constitutional power to perform jobs suggested but not directly stated in the Constitution.
Gibbons v. Ogden	1824	Congress's power to make laws about trade and the movement of goods between states was strengthened.
Dred Scott v. Sandford	1857	African Americans were not citizens of the United States, and the Missouri Compromise was unconstitutional.
Plessy v. Ferguson	1896	Racial segregation was constitutional as long as people had access to "separate-but-equal" facilities.
Miranda v. Arizona	1966	People must be told of their constitutional rights when being arrested.
Tinker v. Des Moines	1968	Students have the right to freedom of speech on school grounds.

Landmark Supreme Court Decisions

UNIT 3 / LESSON 6

Interpreting Sources: *United States v. Nixon*

In 1972, a group of burglars broke into the Democratic Party's headquarters in the Watergate building in Washington, D.C. Over the next several months, it became clear that Republican campaigners were involved in the break-in. These Republicans were working for the re-election efforts of President Richard M. Nixon. Nixon claimed he had no involvement with the burglary. He also said he had not allowed the White House to try to cover up the involvement of the Republican Party in the burglary. Politicians, citizens, and the media began to question Nixon's statements.

Congress held hearings to look into the scandal. A Congressional committee learned that Nixon had recorded conversations in his office. The committee asked Nixon for the tapes. He refused, saying that they were protected by **executive privilege**. Executive privilege is the president's right to keep some information secret in the interests of national security. The issue went to the Supreme Court. The Court issued its opinion in *United States v. Nixon* in 1974.

> Neither the doctrine of separation of powers nor the generalized need for confidentiality of high-level communications, without more, can sustain an absolute, unqualified Presidential privilege of immunity from judicial process under all circumstances. . . . the confidentiality of Presidential communications is not significantly diminished by producing material for a criminal trial under . . . protected conditions. . . .
>
> [W]hen a claim of Presidential privilege . . . is based, as it is here, not on the ground that military or diplomatic secrets are implicated, but merely on the ground of a generalized interest in confidentiality, the President's generalized assertion of privilege must yield to the demonstrated, specific need for evidence in a pending criminal trial and the fundamental demands of due process of law in the fair administration of criminal justice. . . .

The opinion refers to an important constitutional idea—separation of powers. The Court is basing its decision on its interpretation of the Constitution.

The Court agrees that the president has the right to keep some information secret. However, the Court does not agree that this right is in effect all the time. Giving up information to Congress, which agrees to keep sensitive information secret, is not always protected.

This opinion was an important check on the president's power. The Court said that executive privilege had certain limits.

Lesson Practice

Complete the activities below to check your understanding of the lesson content.

Vocabulary

Write complete sentences to answer each question that follows.

1. What were two effects of the Judiciary Act of 1789?

   _____

   _____

2. How are judicial review and judicial activism different?

   _____

   _____

3. What is the purpose of executive privilege?

   _____

   _____

Lesson Practice

UNIT 3 / LESSON 6

Apply Your Knowledge

Complete the graphic organizer using the case bank. You will use one of the cases twice.

McCulloch v. Maryland
Gibbons v. Ogden
Dred Scott v. Sandford
Plessy v. Ferguson

Miranda v. Arizona
Tinker v. Des Moines
United States v. Nixon

4. Two cases that mostly grew Congressional power: _____ _____	5. Two cases that mostly limited the executive branch's powers: _____ _____
6. Two cases that set precedents no longer in use today: _____ _____	7. Two cases that mostly protected individual rights: _____ _____

KEY POINT!

The U.S. Supreme Court is the most powerful court in the United States. It has the job of interpreting the Constitution.

UNIT 3 / LESSON 6

Lesson Practice

Skills Practice

Read the text. Then choose the correct answer to each question.

The U.S. Supreme Court decision in *Brown v. Board of Education of Topeka, Kansas*, had an immense effect on life in the United States. Public schools in Kansas and certain other states were segregated by race, and all-white public schools in these states denied admission to otherwise qualified African American students. The NAACP, a civil rights organization, filed lawsuits for some of these students in the early 1950s. Three federal courts ruled against the students. They stated that the Supreme Court's decision in *Plessy v. Ferguson* permitted segregated schools. But one federal court ruled for the students. This court said that African American schools were rarely actually equal to all-white schools, so the practice was unconstitutional.

In 1954, the Supreme Court agreed to settle the issue. It discussed all four court rulings at the same time. The Court considered whether segregation was constitutional according to the Fourteenth Amendment. This amendment requires equal protection under the law for all people. Chief Justice Earl Warren wrote the Court's opinion. He said that separating people by race made African American students feel unequal to white students. He also argued that segregation made it harder for all people to learn about one another. All the justices agreed, and segregation in public schools was overturned.

8. Based on this passage, what conclusion about the Supreme Court is best supported?
   - A The Court lacks the ability to overturn earlier decisions.
   - B The Court has the authority to hear cases begun in the states.
   - C Few cases heard by the Court involve national issues.
   - D Justices must unanimously agree on its decisions.

9. Based on this passage, what inference about the NAACP is best supported?
   - A The NAACP opposed the outcome of *Plessy v. Ferguson*.
   - B Most NAACP members were African Americans.
   - C The NAACP opposed the language of the Fourteenth Amendment.
   - D Members of the NAACP usually attended public schools.

10. Which of these was specifically banned by the decision in *Brown v. Board of Education of Topeka, Kansas*?
    - A making people of different races use separate entrances and exits to public buildings
    - B requiring African Americans to use separate textbooks and classrooms in the same school
    - C keeping books about subjects of interest to African Americans in special library sections
    - D forcing children of different races to attend different public schools

See page 143 for answers and help.

TEST STRATEGY

Read answer choices carefully in order to avoid making careless mistakes. Read the choices for Question 9. Notice that both A and C refer to possible things opposed by the NAACP. The text suggests that the organization opposed one of these but likely supported the other. Reading the choices too quickly might make you mix up these options.

Elections

UNIT 3 / LESSON 7

Role of Political Parties

No **political parties** existed when the United States was founded. George Washington and other national founders thought parties were a threat to liberty. A political party is an organized group that supports a set of political beliefs. However, leaders and citizens disagreed on certain issues even in the early days of the republic. Supporters of a strong federal government and loose interpretation of the Constitution formed one party. Supporters of strong state governments and strict interpretation of the Constitution formed another. Today, the two major political parties are the **Democratic Party** and the **Republican Party**. The Democratic Party traces its roots to the 1790s. The Republican Party was formed as an anti-slavery party. It began soon before the Civil War.

The main job of political parties is to nominate **candidates** for elections. A candidate is a person who runs for a political office. Political parties also develop **platforms**. A platform tells what ideals and goals the party has. Each ideal or goal is called a plank.

The Election Process

The first official step in most elections is the **primary election**. The primary election allows voters of a certain political party to say which candidate they want to run. Several candidates from the same party may run in a primary election. The winner usually goes on to be the party's candidate in the **general election**. Registered voters may vote for anyone they wish in the general election rather than just candidates within their own party.

Candidates use **campaigns** to try to persuade voters to vote for them. Campaigns may include public speeches, television commercials, websites, debates, and other tools to reach citizens. Campaigns can be very expensive, especially for national offices like Congress or the presidency. Political parties help raise money for their candidates. So do special fundraising groups.

KEY WORDS

- campaign
- candidate
- Democratic Party
- Electoral College
- general election
- platform
- political party
- primary election
- Republican Party

UNIT 3 / LESSON 7 — Elections

Interpreting Sources: Electoral College

The **Electoral College** is a group of special voters who choose the president. Review the following passage to learn more about the Electoral College.

> The U.S. Constitution created the Electoral College as the official way to choose the president and vice president. At that time, it was extremely difficult for citizens to gather and cast votes for president all at the same time. The Electoral College allowed state legislatures and political parties to make decisions about which candidate should receive their state's support.
>
> Over time, however, the method of choosing electors has changed. During the 1820s, citizens began casting a direct vote for president by picking which electors to support. However, the citizens' direct votes—known as the popular vote—do not necessarily choose the president. Each state except for Maine and Nebraska tells its electors to all vote for the candidate who won the most votes in the state. This means that a candidate may win 51% of citizens' vote but receive 100% support from the state's electors.
>
> Occasionally, a presidential candidate who wins the popular vote nationwide does not win the election. The candidate might have received big majorities in some states and lost others by relatively few votes. The possibility of misrepresentation is the greatest limit of the Electoral College system.

Annotations:

- This paragraph explains the reasons for the creation of the Electoral College. It was designed to fix the problem of how to elect the president. However, this solution had limits. It did not easily allow regular voters to have a direct say on the office.

- The Electoral College changed over time. These changes revealed a new limit on the process: state votes may not fairly represent those of each voter.

- The text ends with an opinion: that misrepresentation is the greatest limit of the Electoral College system. Notice that, to support this opinion, the author includes facts about elections that may have misrepresented voters' wishes.

Lesson Practice

UNIT 3 / LESSON 7

Complete the activities below to check your understanding of the lesson content.

Vocabulary

Match the term on the left with the correct definition on the right.

1. candidate

   A. major political party with roots in the 1790s

2. Democratic Party

   B. list of a political party's ideals and goals

3. Electoral College

   C. an organized group that supports a set of political beliefs

4. platform

   D. person running for political office

5. political party

   E. major political party founded shortly before the Civil War

6. Republican Party

   F. group of special voters who choose the president

KEY POINT!

Political parties influence the nation's government by nominating candidates and running campaigns.

Lesson Practice

Skills Practice

Study the map. Then choose the correct answer to each question.

Election of 1960

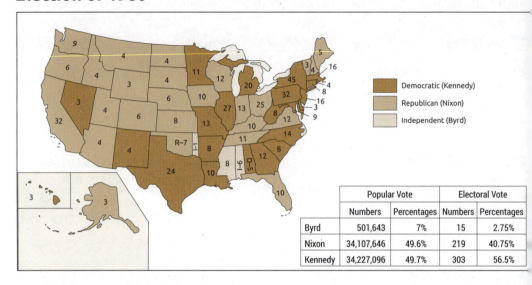

7. What percentage of the popular vote did Kennedy receive?

   A 40.75

   B 49.6

   C 49.7

   D 56.6

8. One elector from Oklahoma voted for an independent candidate. Suppose this elector had instead voted with the rest of the electors from his state. Would this have changed the outcome of the election?

   A No, because Kennedy had many more electoral votes than Nixon.

   B No, because Oklahoma has few electoral votes.

   C Yes, because the popular vote was so close.

   D Yes, because Nixon would have carried more states than Kennedy.

See page 144 for answers and help.

TEST STRATEGY

Review graphics and maps carefully to find information. Remember to check the map legend to help you identify specific pieces of information. Read Question 7. This question asks you to find the percentage of the popular vote received by Kennedy. Find this information on the map legend. Be careful to match up the right answer with what you find.

Special Interest Groups

UNIT 3 / LESSON 8

Working for Goals

Lawmakers of the U.S. Congress get ideas for laws from many sources. **Special interest groups** are one source of ideas for lawmakers. These are groups of citizens who work together for a common goal. For example, a group like the Sierra Club, which wants the United States to have protected wilderness areas, is a special interest group. AARP is a special interest group supporting policies that help older Americans. Expanding rights, protecting business interests, or creating social changes are all common goals of special interest groups.

Special interest groups may employ **lobbyists** to work for laws and policies. Lobbyists are people who try to persuade government leaders to support the goals of a special interest group. They often build close relationships with lawmakers. Special interest groups also work to build public interest in their goals. These groups may advertise on television or convince journalists to write news stories.

Some special interest groups give large amounts of money to political campaigns. They may fundraise for candidates who share their goals. To do so, special interest groups usually form **political action committees (PACs)**. A PAC is an organization dedicated to raising money for a particular candidate or cause. In 2010, the U.S. Supreme Court issued a ruling that created a new kind of PAC called a **super PAC**. Super PACs can raise and spend unlimited amounts of money. However, they cannot donate directly to a candidate.

KEY WORDS

- lobbyist
- political action committee (PAC)
- special interest group
- super PAC

UNIT 3 / LESSON 8

Lesson Practice

KEY POINT!

Special interest groups work toward goals through lobbying, advertising, and political support.

Complete the activities below to check your understanding of the lesson content.

Vocabulary

Write definitions in your own words for each of the key terms.

1. lobbyist _____

   _____

2. political action committee (PAC) _____

   _____

3. special interest group _____

   _____

4. super PAC _____

   _____

Skills Practice

Read the following text from a television commercial. Then choose the correct answer to each question.

> Americans agree that this Congress is one of the worst in history. It's time to shake up the system. Let's send a message to Washington. Choose new voices for America! This message was paid for by the Election Fund for Tomorrow.

5. Based on this passage, what is the main goal of the Election Fund for Tomorrow?
   - **A** to help the re-election efforts of certain Congress people
   - **B** to raise money for a trip to Washington
   - **C** to convince voters to pick new members of Congress
   - **D** to suggest candidates for national office

6. What bias does this advertisement show?
   - **A** a bias toward a political party
   - **B** a bias against current members of Congress
   - **C** a bias toward young voters
   - **D** a bias against Washington

See page 144 for answers and help.

TEST STRATEGY

Summarize the passage to find its main idea. Review this passage. You might summarize it as *Elect new Congress members*. Now, read Question 5. How does your summary help you answer this question?

Citizenship

UNIT 3 / LESSON 9

Rights and Responsibilities of Citizenship

A **citizen** is a person who is a legal member of a place. U.S. citizenship has both privileges and responsibilities. Citizens have the right to live and work in the United States. They can vote in elections for local, state, and national leaders. They also have access to many government programs and benefits. In return, citizens support their country. They vote in elections, serve on juries, and pay taxes. They might also fight in the military if asked to serve.

Naturalization Process

Immigrants to the United States who meet certain conditions may apply for citizenship. An immigrant is someone who moves to a country in order to live there. People first apply to become permanent residents of the United States. Permanent residents have the right to live and work in the United States, but they are not yet citizens. After several years, permanent residents may follow the **naturalization** process. Naturalization is becoming a citizen of a new place.

People must follow steps to become naturalized citizens. They apply to the government using a special form. Then they are interviewed and may have their fingerprints taken. The federal agency in charge of immigration decides whether to approve the application. People whose applications are approved take an oath of allegiance to the United States. After taking this oath, people are U.S. citizens.

KEY WORDS

- citizen
- immigrant
- naturalization

Citizenship

Interpreting Sources: Viewpoints on Citizenship

The DREAM Act was first introduced in 2001. In 2012, President Barack Obama asked the U.S. Congress to pass it again. This law would allow young people who entered the United States illegally as children to pursue citizenship. Young people would have to meet certain standards, such as graduating from school and avoiding breaking any laws, to be considered. The DREAM Act is very controversial. People disagree on whether those who came to the United States without permission should be able to receive the privileges of citizenship.

Newspaper X

The United States is a nation of immigrants! Welcoming people from around the world is part of our heritage. Americans should support government policies that give young immigrants a path to citizenship. These children and young adults may have entered the United States without following legal processes. But they have often spent much of their lives in the United States. They share our dreams, values, and ideals. Helping them stay in the country they love will benefit all Americans.

> This newspaper supports expanding opportunities for citizenship. It says that people should support a path to citizenship. It gives claims and opinions in favor of this viewpoint.

> Both paragraphs give viewpoints about immigration and citizenship.

Newspaper Y

Why should we welcome lawbreakers to the United States? Our country already has more than 300 million residents. More than 13 million of those people are non-citizens who entered the country legally and received permission to stay permanently. Making it easy for people who did not follow the rules to get citizenship is unfair to the millions of people who have. It will encourage others to try to get around the law, too. Don't we have enough Americans to take care of already?

> This newspaper opposes expanding opportunities for citizenship. It argues that this would be unfair to those already in the country legally. It gives claims and examples to try to persuade readers to oppose this policy.

Lesson Practice

UNIT 3 / LESSON 9

Complete the activities below to check your understanding of the lesson content.

Vocabulary

Complete each sentence with the correct term from the lesson.

1. Rosa's grandmother is a(n) _____ because she moved to Texas from where she was born in Mexico.

2. Mr. Lee applied recently to begin _____ since he wants to become a citizen.

3. A (n) _____ has a duty to help his or her country in times of need.

Skills Practice

Categorize each of the following as a right *or* responsibility *of citizenship. One will be both a right and a responsibility.*

4. joining the military _____

5. working in a place _____

6. serving on juries _____

7. paying taxes _____

8. voting _____

9. using some government services _____

KEY POINT!

Citizenship has both rights and responsibilities. People can become citizens by completing the naturalization process.

UNIT 3 / LESSON 9

Lesson Practice

Study the steps. Then choose the correct answer to each question.

Naturalization Eligibility Requirements

- Be at least 18 years old
- Have lived continuously in the United States as a permanent resident for at least 5 years
- Have lived in the state where you apply for at least 3 months
- Be able to read, write, and speak some English
- Understand basic U.S. history and government
- Have good moral character and support the ideals of the U.S. Constitution

10. Which of the following would prevent a person from being able to apply for naturalization?
    A   speaking Spanish at home
    B   participating in a political protest
    C   studying something other than history in college
    D   having spent the last year living in China for work

11. Supporters of the DREAM Act would most likely support removing which of the following requirements from this list?
    A   Be at least 18 years old
    B   Have lived continuously in the United States as a permanent resident for at least 5 years
    C   Have lived in the state where you apply for at least 3 months
    D   Have good moral character and support the ideals of the U.S. Constitution

See page 144 for answers and help.

TEST STRATEGY

Use the process of elimination to help answer questions like Question 11. Think about what you know about the DREAM Act. Check each answer choice to see if it matches with the goals and ideas of the Act. Eliminate answer choices that would likely be requirements for citizenship according to this law.

State and Local Government

UNIT 3 / LESSON 10

KEY WORDS
- council-manager system
- governor
- mayor-council system
- municipal government

State Government

Remember that the United States uses a federal system that divides power between the states and the national government. Each state has its own independent government with the authority to oversee certain government jobs. States build roads, run school systems, and issue licenses, for example. They also can change taxes, including income tax and sales tax.

State governments are set up by state constitutions. Like the national government, state governments have three branches. The head of a state's executive branch is called the **governor**. Other jobs in the executive branch may include the attorney general, who is the top lawyer, and the secretary of state, who often oversees elections. States also have legislatures that are mostly modeled after the U.S. Congress. One state, Nebraska, has a legislature with only one house. State courts try cases related to state laws.

Municipal Government

State governments grant some powers to local, or municipal governments. **Municipal governments** usually include many levels. Counties, parishes, or boroughs can all establish their own governments. Communities within counties also set up city, town, or village governments. Municipal governments employ police officers and firefighters. They may work with state governments to operate schools and libraries. They also oversee city services like water, trash removal, and road maintenance. City or county courts hear local trials. Cities and counties also manage property deeds and other day-to-day government activities.

Municipal governments can include special districts. School districts are one common type of special district. Wards, recreation districts, and other divisions also exist.

UNIT 3 / LESSON 10 — State and Local Government

Interpreting Sources: Forms of Local Government

The two most widely used forms of local government in the United States are the **mayor-council system** and the **council-manager system**. The mayor-council system has an elected mayor who acts as the head of the city's executive branch. An elected local council makes laws and policies. The council-manager system also has a council, which hires a paid, professional city manager to run the city's regular business.

> This paragraph gives information that is important to reading the table. The first sentence of the paragraph gives the main idea. The rest of the paragraph gives details that tell about that idea.

Local Governments in Ten Most Populous U.S. Cities

City	Population (2014 est.)	Form of Local Government
New York, NY	8,491,079	Mayor-Council
Los Angeles, CA	3,928,864	Mayor-Council
Chicago, IL	2,722,389	Mayor-Council
Houston, TX	2,239,558	Mayor-Council
Philadelphia, PA	1,560,297	Mayor-Council
Phoenix, AZ	1,537,058	Council-Manager
San Antonio, TX	1,436,697	Council-Manager
San Diego, CA	1,381,069	Mayor-Council
Dallas, TX	1,281,047	Council-Manager
San Jose, CA	1,015,785	Council-Manager

> This section of the table lists the ten most populous cities and gives their populations. Notice the significant gap between the most populous city, New York, and the second-most popular, Los Angeles. Several cities have populations between 1 and 2 million.

> This section of the table tells what kind of government each city has. Six of the cities have a mayor-council system, and the rest use a council-manager system. Look for other patterns. The cities with a council-manager system, for example, are in the South and West.

Lesson Practice

UNIT 3 / LESSON 10

Complete the activities below to check your understanding of the lesson content.

Vocabulary

Choose the correct answer to each question.

1. What is the name of the office that heads a state's executive branch?
   A attorney general
   B governor
   C president
   D secretary of state

2. Which of these is a municipal government?
   A national government of the United States
   B government of the state of Nevada
   C student government of Las Vegas High School
   D government of Clark County, Nevada

3. What is one similarity between the council-manager system and the mayor-council system?
   A Both have elected members of the legislative branch.
   B Both rely on hired professionals to manage day-to-day affairs.
   C Both are used in the nation's three most populous cities.
   D Both have become less popular over time.

TEST STRATEGY

Categorize each answer choice as true or false to help you find correct choices. Read the choices for Question 2. Ask yourself whether it is true or false that this is a type of municipal, or local, government. Eliminate each choice that you categorize as false.

UNIT 3 / LESSON 10

Lesson Practice

KEY POINT!

State governments are organized by constitutions and have certain powers. Local governments provide everyday services like water and public safety.

Skills Practice

Read the passage. Then write complete sentences to answer the questions that follow.

The city of Galveston, Texas, was struck by a devastating hurricane in 1900. Thousands of people were injured or killed. Homes, businesses, roads, and public buildings were all destroyed. Citizens of Galveston worried that the city would struggle to rebuild. This natural disaster led to the creation of a new type of municipal government in 1901.

A group of prominent Galveston residents asked the Texas governor to appoint a commission to run Galveston while it recovered from the storm. Galveston's commission would have five members. One member would act as the mayor. The other commissioners would oversee specific city services, like police and fire safety. Supporters thought the commission system would be stronger and more decisive than the city's existing mayor-council system. Each commissioner would have the power to make choices quickly and efficiently for his area.

Galveston soon changed its plan so that the commissioners were elected instead of appointed. In this form, the commission system began to spread. Houston adopted a commission system in 1905. Other cities followed. Some cities—including Galveston—eventually switched over to a council-manager system, introduced a few years later. Portland, Oregon, is the most populous city to use the commission system today.

4. What sentence from the text gives the main idea of the first paragraph?

___

5. The second paragraph makes this claim: *Supporters thought the commission system would be stronger and more decisive than the city's existing mayor-council system.* What detail in the second paragraph supports this idea?

___

6. What is the main idea of the third paragraph? Write it in your own words.

___

See page 144 for answers and help.

Government Documents

UNIT 3 / LESSON 11

KEY WORDS

- functional document
- voter registration form

Documents and Forms

You may already be familiar with some functional documents. A **functional document** is any kind of form people complete as part of a task. For example, job applications, drivers' license forms, and tax forms are all types of functional documents. The Civics & Government section of the HiSET® often includes questions about reading and understanding government documents like these.

All these government documents have similarities. They will ask for your name and other identifying details. They require close reading to ensure that you add the right information. Filling out a form incorrectly may mean that it is not accepted. Always take your time and write clearly when filling out a government document.

Follow these steps to read and complete a government document:

Step 1: Read the instructions on the form carefully. Refer to them as often as you need when completing the document.

Step 2: Fill out the information in each box. Sometimes a box will not apply to you. You can leave boxes like these blank.

Step 3: Write neatly and carefully. Use your best spelling. If you need to add or subtract numbers, use a calculator to ensure accuracy.

Step 4: Review the completed form. Look for mistakes or missing information.

UNIT 3 / LESSON 11 — Government Documents

Interpreting Sources: Voter Registration Form

People complete forms regularly. One important government form is a **voter registration form**. This is the document people use to add their names to the voter rolls in their communities. People can register to vote at local boards of elections. They may also find forms online, at local libraries, or at other offices. This form is a national form that can be used to register anywhere.

> States make their own specific voting laws. This form is a national form, so in order to fill it out correctly, the potential voter must read the directions about his or her state.

> Notice the two questions in this corner. A person under the age of 18 is not eligible to register to vote. Neither is a person who is over 18 but is not a citizen of the United States.

Voter Registration Application
Before completing this form, review the General, Application, and State specific instructions.

Are you a citizen of the United States of America? ☐ Yes ☐ No
Will you be 18 years old on or before election day? ☐ Yes ☐ No
If you checked "No" in response to either of these questions, do not complete form.
(Please see state-specific instructions for rules regarding eligibility to register prior to age 18.)

This space for office use only.

1. ☐ Mr. ☐ Miss ☐ Mrs. ☐ Ms. | Last Name | First Name | Middle Name(s) | ☐ Jr ☐ Sr ☐ II ☐ III ☐ IV

2. Home Address | Apt. or Lot # | City/Town | State | Zip Code

3. Address Where You Get Your Mail If Different From Above | City/Town | State | Zip Code

4. Date of Birth — Month Day Year
5. Telephone Number (optional)
6. ID Number – (See item 6 in the instructions for your state)

7. Choice of Party (see item 7 in the instructions for your State)
8. Race or Ethnic Group (see item 8 in the instructions for your State)

9. I have reviewed my state's instructions and I swear/affirm that:
- I am a United States citizen
- I meet the eligibility requirements of my state and subscribe to any oath required.
- The information I have provided is true to the best of my knowledge under penalty of perjury. If I have provided false information, I may be fined, imprisoned, or (if not a U.S. citizen) deported from or refused entry to the United States.

Please sign full name (or put mark) ▲

Date: Month / Day / Year

If you are registering to vote for the first time: please refer to the application instructions for information on submitting copies of valid identification documents with this form.

> This section gives people the chance to share more than one address. Suppose your sister attends a college in a neighboring state. She could add her parents' address here as her main address but include her mailing address at college, too.

Lesson Practice

UNIT 3 / LESSON 11

Complete the activities below to check your understanding of the lesson content.

Apply Your Knowledge

Write the correct order of the four steps using the letters A, B, C, and D. Then write complete sentences to answer the question that follows.

1. Step _____	Fill out the information in each box. Sometimes a box will not apply to you. You can leave boxes like these blank.
2. Step _____	Read the instructions on the form carefully. Refer to them as often as you need when completing the document.
3. Step _____	Review the completed form. Look for mistakes or missing information.
4. Step _____	Write neatly and carefully. Use your best spelling. If you need to add or subtract numbers, use a calculator to ensure accuracy.

5. What is one more suggestion you can think of for reading and interpreting government forms?

_____

_____

_____

_____

_____

_____

KEY POINT!

Understanding government documents relies on close and careful reading skills.

Lesson Practice

Skills Practice

Review the document. Then choose the correct answer to each question.

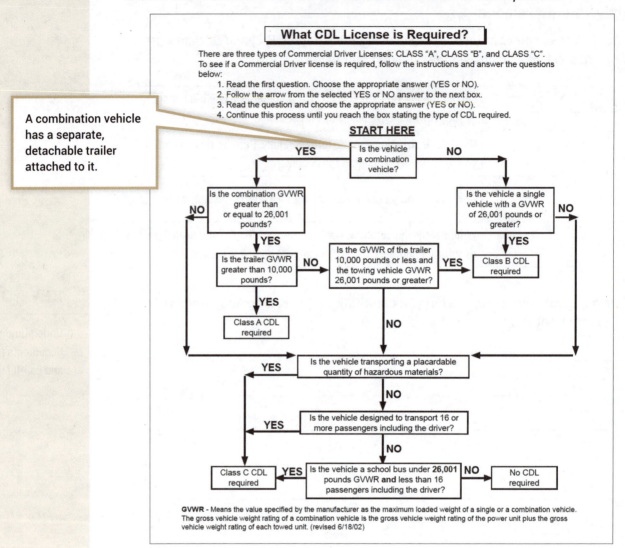

TEST STRATEGY

When you read a flow chart, first read the information at the top and bottom of the chart. Then find the starting place. Read Question 6. You can find the answer by following the flow chart.

6. What kind of CDL does the driver of a standard-sized school bus with a GVWR of 25,400 pounds and seating up to 72 passengers need?

   A   Class A CDL
   B   Class B CDL
   C   Class C CDL
   D   No CDL is needed.

7. According to the chart, how is the GVWR of a combination vehicle calculated?

   A   by adding the gross vehicle weight rating of all parts of the vehicle
   B   by measuring just the gross vehicle weight rating of the power unit
   C   by subtracting the gross vehicle weight rating of the power unit from the trailers
   D   by comparing the gross vehicle weight rating of the loaded and unloaded trailers

See page 144 for answers and help.

Unit Test — UNIT 3

Answer the questions based on the content covered in this unit.

1. The government of Turkey is led by a prime minister and a president. Citizens elect leaders who make laws and policies for them in government. Turkey is most likely a
   - A communist state.
   - B direct democracy.
   - C republic.
   - D theocracy.

Read the following text, taken from the Federalist No. 14. *Then answer questions 2 and 3.*

> In the first place it is to be remembered that the general government is not to be charged with the whole power of making and administering laws. Its jurisdiction is limited to certain [listed] objects, which concern all the members of the republic, but which are not to be attained by the separate provisions of any. The [lower] governments, which can extend their care to all those other subjects which can be separately provided for, will retain their due authority and activity. Were it proposed by the plan of the convention to abolish the governments of the particular States, its [opponents] would have some ground for their objection; though it would not be difficult to show that if they were abolished the general government would be compelled, by the principle of self-preservation, to reinstate them in their proper jurisdiction. . . .

2. Which constitutional principle is best described in this excerpt?
   - A federalism
   - B popular sovereignty
   - C separation of powers
   - D individual rights

3. Based on this passage, which inference about opponents to the Constitution is best supported?
   - A They disliked the creation of the office of the presidency.
   - B They were mostly political leaders in the state governments.
   - C They wished to make substantial changes to the Articles of Confederation.
   - D They believed the Constitution would too greatly weaken state power.

4. Which of the following people is NOT a member of the legislative branch?
   - A vice president
   - B Speaker of the House
   - C majority whip
   - D state governor

Read the following excerpt from a speech given by President James Monroe in 1823. Then answer question 5.

> In the discussions to which this interest has given rise and in the arrangements by which they may terminate the occasion has been judged proper for asserting, as a principle in which the rights and interests of the United States are involved, that the American continents, by the free and independent condition which they have assumed and maintain, are henceforth not to be considered as subjects for future colonization by any European powers. . .

5. President Monroe gave this speech to Congress as part of an annual address. Which presidential duty does this speech most reflect?
   - A leading the nation's military
   - B making treaties and setting foreign policy
   - C naming members of the Cabinet
   - D suggesting laws for passage by Congress

UNIT 3 — Unit Test

Read the following excerpt, taken from the U.S. Supreme Court opinion in Dred Scott v. Sandford, *issued in 1856. Then, answer questions 6–8.*

> 5. When the Constitution was adopted, [African Americans] were not regarded in any of the States as members of the community which constituted the State, and were not numbered among its "people or citizens." Consequently, the special rights and immunities guaranteed to citizens do not apply to them. And not being "citizens" within the meaning of the Constitution, they are not entitled to sue in that character in a court of the United States, and the Circuit Court has not jurisdiction in such a suit.
>
> 6. The only two clauses in the Constitution which point to this race treat them as persons whom it was morally lawfully to deal in as articles of property and to hold as slaves.
>
> 7. Since the adoption of the Constitution of the United States, no State can by any subsequent law make a foreigner or any other description of persons citizens of the United States, nor entitle them to the rights and privileges secured to citizens by that instrument.
>
> 8. A State, by its laws passed since the adoption of the Constitution, may put a foreigner or any other description of persons upon a footing with its own citizens as to all the rights and privileges enjoyed by them within its dominion and by its laws. But that will not make him a citizen of the United States, nor entitle him to sue in its courts, nor to any of the privileges and immunities of a citizen in another State.

6. Which Constitutional amendment overturned this opinion?
   - A Thirteenth Amendment, which abolished slavery
   - B Fourteenth Amendment, which established birthright citizenship
   - C. Fifteenth Amendment, which gave African Americans the right to vote
   - D Twenty-Fourth Amendment, which ended discriminatory voting practices

7. According to this opinion, why could the legislative branch not ban slavery?
   - A African Americans were instead required to sue for freedom.
   - B Only states had the right to make laws to this effect.
   - C The Constitution treated African Americans as property.
   - D Such a change fell under the process of judicial review.

8. Based on this passage, what was one other person who could not claim U.S. citizenship?
   - A an immigrant from Ireland who resided in New York
   - B a woman born after the writing of the Constitution
   - C a man who refused to serve in the U.S. military
   - D a child under the age of 18 who could not yet vote

Use the following map to answer questions 9–11.

Election of 1860

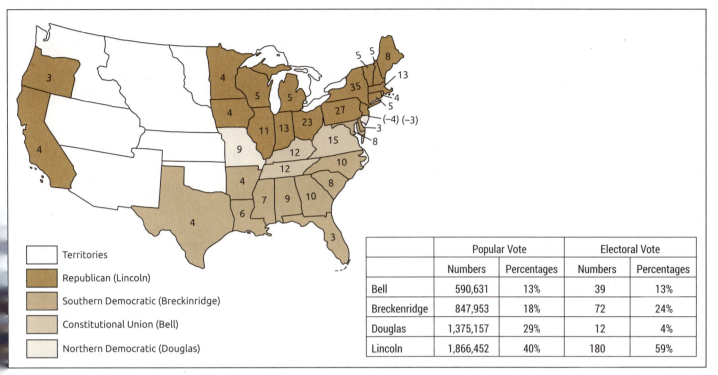

9. Southern opponents of Lincoln complained that his election in 1860 did not represent their interests. Based on the map, which statement best supports this claim?

    A Lincoln's support came only from free states.

    B Douglas won the electoral vote in only one state that permitted slavery.

    C Support for Lincoln was scattered all across the country.

    D Four major candidates received support in the Electoral College.

10. Which candidate won the second-highest number of votes in the Electoral College?

    A Bell
    B Breckinridge
    C Douglas
    D Lincoln

11. Why are no electoral votes recorded for places like Utah and New Mexico?

    A These places had already seceded from the United States.

    B Only states that had majorities for Lincoln or Douglas were counted.

    C The vote in these places was indecisive.

    D Territories are not included in the Electoral College vote.

Refer to the following political cartoon to answer question 12.

"Time to rake up the leaflets."

12. With which statement would the creator of this cartoon probably agree?

   A Not enough qualified candidates are running for office today.

   B Changes to voting laws make it too hard for some people to vote.

   C Special interest groups make elections too expensive and complicated.

   D Americans should have to pass tests to prove they are knowledgeable before voting.

See page 144 for answers and help.

Read the following text from the U.S. Constitution. Then answer questions 13 and 14.

Amendment XIV

Section 1.

All persons born or naturalized in the United States, and subject to the jurisdiction thereof, are citizens of the United States and of the state wherein they reside. No state shall make or enforce any law which shall abridge the privileges or immunities of citizens of the United States; nor shall any state deprive any person of life, liberty, or property, without due process of law; nor deny to any person within its jurisdiction the equal protection of the laws.

13. According to this amendment, which person is NOT necessarily a U.S. citizen?

   A an African American born in the United States

   B the foreign-born wife of a native-born U.S. citizen

   C an immigrant who has completed the naturalization process

   D a child of immigrants who was born in the United States

14. Based on this amendment, which conclusion about the Constitution is best supported?

   A The Constitution did not originally include a definition of citizenship.

   B The Constitution originally restricted citizenship to property-owning men.

   C The Constitution was originally written mostly to explain how the states should act.

   D The Constitution had originally required the states to decide how to define citizenship.

Unit Answer Key — UNIT 3

Lesson 1
1. A. Lords are referred to as the "landed elite."
2. B. The "strong centralized government" was ruled by an emperor.
3. B. Emperors and kings were the official leaders, despite the strong power held by landowners.
4. D. See the Test Strategy for more help on this item.

Lesson 2
1. colonial era; set up a form of self-government
2. American Revolution; rejected the rule of the British king, established key democratic principles
3. Early Republic; first plan for national government
4. Early Republic; explained constitutional ideals and worked for adoption of the Constitution
5. A. Adding the Bill of Rights increased support for the Constitution.
6. D. Some leaders thought the Constitution gave too much power to the federal government. The Bill of Rights protects the rights of the people.
7. B. See the Test Strategy for more help on this item.

Lesson 3
1. A.
2. B. See the Test Strategy for more help on this item.

Lesson 4
1. law-making body with two houses. A clue to the meaning of *bicameral* is its root, *bi*, meaning *two*.
2. proposed law
3. national legislature created by the Constitution
4. one house of U.S. Congress with lots of members
5. one house of U.S. Congress with two members from each state
6. head of the majority party in the House of Representatives
7. C.
8. D. See the Test Strategy for more help on this item.

Lesson 5
1. B. If you are looking for answer choices you can quickly eliminate, think about the choices logically. The president does not choose a cabinet until after an election. It does not make sense for the Cabinet to help a president get elected.
2. D. See the Test Strategy for more help on this item.
3. A. You can eliminate the other choices, since they are all untrue.
4. C. Jackson was a strong leader who sometimes acted more like a king than an elected president.
5. Sample answer: The artist is suggesting that it will be hard for Jackson to overcome Congress. It is a strong and powerful creature.
6. Sample answer: I think the artist views Jackson negatively. He is shown fighting a battle he probably cannot win.

Lesson 6
1. The Judiciary Act of 1789 set up the U.S. Supreme Court. It also established a series of lower federal courts.
2. Judicial review is the Supreme Court's power to decide whether something is constitutional. Judicial activism, however, is the use of the Court's power to make change happen in laws or society.
3. Executive privilege is the president's right to keep certain information secret. It is used to protect national security or meet other national interests. The Court said it cannot be used for a president's personal benefit. Keep in mind that the Executive Branch includes the president, so questions including *executive* might have something to do with the president's responsibilities or powers.
4. *McCulloch v. Maryland* and *Gibbons v. Ogden*
5. *Miranda v. Arizona* and *United States v. Nixon* Remember that the executive branch includes the parts of government that enforce laws. Police are part of the executive branch because they enforce laws. The requirement of *Miranda v. Arizona* that police tell suspects their constitutional rights can limit the executive branch's power over suspects.
6. *Dred Scott v. Sandford* and *Plessy v. Ferguson* The Fourteenth Amendment affirmed African Americans' citizenship. Later Court decisions and federal laws ended the idea of "separate but equal."
7. *Miranda v. Arizona* and *Tinker v. Des Moines*
8. B.
9. A. See the Test Strategy for more help on this item.
10. D.

Lesson 7
1. D.
2. A.
3. F.
4. B.
5. C.
6. E.
7. C. See the Test Strategy for more help on this item.
8. A. Compare the numbers of electoral votes for each candidate in the table.

Lesson 8
1. someone who tries to persuade government leaders to support the goals of a special interest group
2. an organization that raises money for a particular candidate or cause
3. a group of citizens who work together for a common goal
4. an organization that can raise and spend unlimited amounts of money
5. C. See the Test Strategy for more help on this item.

UNIT 3 Unit Answer Key

6. B.

Lesson 9

1. immigrant
2. naturalization
3. citizen
4. responsibility
5. right
6. responsibility
7. responsibility
8. right and responsibility
9. right
10. D.
11. B. See the Test Strategy for more help on this item.

Lesson 10

1. B.
2. D. See the Test Strategy for more help on this item.
3. A. In both cases, local council members are elected.
4. The city of Galveston, Texas, was struck by a devastating hurricane in 1900.
5. Each commissioner would have the power to make choices quickly and efficiently for his area.
6. Sample answer: The commission system got more popular over time, but it is not used much today.

Lesson 11

1. B.
2. A.
3. D.
4. C.
5. Sample answer: Read the title carefully to make sure you choose the right document.
6. C. See the Test Strategy for more help on this item.
7. A. The note below the flow chart describes how the weight is calculated.

Unit Test

1. C.
2. A.
3. D.
4. D.
5. B.
6. B.
7. C.
8. A.
9. A.
10. B.
11. D.
12. C.
13. B.
14. A.

Unit Glossary — UNIT 3

- **Articles of Confederation** — first governing document of the United States that gave most power to the states
- **bicameral legislature** — law-making body with two houses
- **bill** — proposed law
- **Bill of Rights** — first ten amendments that protect individual and state rights
- **Cabinet** — group of presidential advisers
- **campaign** — efforts by candidates to persuade voters to choose them
- **candidate** — person running for political office
- **charter** — written document setting up a government
- **checks and balances** — way of balancing power among branches so no one becomes too powerful
- **citizen** — a legal member of a place
- **conclusion** — supported idea that goes one step beyond what is in the text
- **Congress** — national legislature
- **Constitution** — plan for government
- **council-manager system** — system of local government in which an elected council hires a professional city manager to run the city's regular business
- **court-packing plan** — unpopular effort by President Franklin D. Roosevelt to change the Supreme Court
- **Democratic Party** — major political party with roots in the 1790s
- **Electoral College** — group of special voters who choose the president
- **executive branch** — branch of government that enforces laws
- **executive privilege** — right of the president to withhold certain secret information
- **federalism** — system of government in which power is spread between national and state or regional units
- **functional document** — any kind of form people complete as part of a task
- **general election** — election in which voters choose candidates for office
- **government** — system of managing a country, region, or community
- **governor** — head of the state's executive branch
- **House of Representatives** — one house of U.S. Congress with many members
- **immigrant** — someone who moves to a country in order to live there
- **inference** — something that is suggested by the facts in the text but not directly stated
- **judicial activism** — using the federal courts to influence laws or social issues
- **judicial branch** — branch of government that interprets laws
- **judicial review** — the Supreme Court's ability to find laws or actions unconstitutional
- **Judiciary Act of 1789** — federal law establishing the Supreme Court and lower court system
- **legislative branch** — branch of government that makes laws
- **lobbyist** — someone who tries to persuade government leaders to support the goals of a special interest group

Unit Glossary

- **mayor-council system** — system of local government with an elected mayor who acts as the head of the city's executive branch
- **municipal government** — local government such as county or city government
- **naturalization** — process of becoming a citizen of a new place
- **platform** — list of a political party's ideals and goals
- **political action committee (PAC)** — an organization that raises money for a particular candidate or cause
- **political party** — an organized group that supports a set of political beliefs
- **precedent** — way of doing things
- **primary election** — election in which voters cast ballots for candidates of one political party
- **Republican Party** — major political party founded shortly before the Civil War
- **Senate** — one house of U.S. Congress with two members from each state
- **Speaker of the House** — head of the majority party in the House of Representatives
- **special interest group** — a group of citizens who work together for a common goal
- **super PAC** — an organization that can raise and spend unlimited amounts of money toward a candidate or cause
- **voter registration form** — document people use to add their names to the voter rolls in their communities

Study More! — UNIT 3

Forms of Government
- Unitary and confederate governments
- Contemporary national world governments
- Justifications for absolute rule and dictatorships

U.S. Founding Documents
- Declaration of Independence
- Articles of Confederation
- Constitutional principles such as popular sovereignty and federalism
- Constitutional compromises
- Federalist Papers

Inferences and Conclusions
- Faults in logic

The U.S. Congress
- Changes in representation
- Drawing Congressional districts
- Majority and minority whips
- Impeachment process

The Changing Role of the President
- Presidential policies and doctrines
- Pocket veto
- War Powers Act
- Actions of specific presidents
- Presidential scandals such as Watergate
- Functions of the Electoral College

Landmark Supreme Court Decisions
- *Gideon v. Wainwright*
- *Griswold v. Connecticut*
- *Korematsu v. United States*
- *Living v. Virginia*
- *Mapp v. Ohio*
- *Regents of the University of California v. Bakke*
- *Roe v. Wade*

Elections
- Beliefs and ideals of different political parties
- Qualifications for candidates
- Role of third parties

Special Interest Groups
- Specific special interest groups

Citizenship
- Fourteenth Amendment
- Immigration laws and policies
- Civic duties
- Volunteerism

State and Local Government
- State laws and courts
- Shared duties of state and federal government
- Town meetings

Government Documents
- Tax forms
- Library card applications
- Benefits applications

UNIT 4

Economics

A small studio apartment usually has a lower rent than its larger neighbors. What other economic factors could affect how much rent a landlord asks for an apartment?

Suppose you are getting ready to find your first apartment on your own. You have a job with a regular paycheck, so you know just how much you can spend each month on rent. When you study the online classified ads for apartments, you probably see big differences in the prices of apartments. Some parts of town are close to shopping and transportation, so people are willing to pay more to live there. Other parts of town may have older buildings that are less expensive. Whatever decision you make, it will be connected to the economic factors that shape how people get what they need and want. Although economics makes up a relatively small portion of the social studies items on the HiSET®, understanding how to connect these concepts to everyday life will help on the test and beyond.

KEY WORDS

- business cycle
- capital
- chart
- command economy
- consumer
- consumer confidence
- consumer price index (CPI)
- data
- demand
- economic indicator
- entrepreneurship
- factor of production
- good
- graph
- gross domestic product (GDP)
- labor
- labor movement
- labor union
- market economy
- market equilibrium
- minimum wage
- mixed economy
- need
- producer
- regulation
- scarcity
- service
- shortage
- supply
- surplus
- table
- traditional economy
- unemployment rate
- Wagner Act
- want

Economic Basics

UNIT 4 / LESSON 1

Supply and Demand

Economics seeks to explain the basic problem of **scarcity**, or the condition of not having enough of something for everyone to have what they want and need. People have certain needs and wants that they try to fill. A **need** is something that must be met in order to survive, like the need for food. A **want** is just that—something that is nice, but not necessary.

People meet needs and wants with **goods** and **services**. Goods are items like books, cars, and computers. Services are things people do for other people, like cutting hair or giving legal help. **Producers** are people who make goods and services. **Consumers** are people who use them. Two important forces shape how producers and consumers interact. **Supply** tells how much of a good or service producers make. **Demand** tells how much consumers are willing to buy. Supply and demand can vary depending on many factors, especially price.

Factors of Production

Producers use **factors of production** to make goods. A factor of production is any resource that is part of creating something. There are four factors of production. Land and other natural resources are one group. **Labor**, or the efforts of workers, is another. The third is **capital**, which includes all the tools and buildings needed to make and sell goods. Machines, computers, storefronts, and cash registers are all capital. The last factor is **entrepreneurship**. Entrepreneurship is the willingness to take risks to start a business. Without entrepreneurs to take a chance on producing goods and services, no new items would ever be made.

Consider how the factors of production come together. Suppose a company is making a T-shirt with your favorite sports team's logo. An entrepreneur has decided that enough people like the team to risk making the shirt. The company uses cotton grown on land to make the shirt. A designer makes a plan for how the shirt will look. A worker sews it together in a garment factory using a sewing machine and thread. Then, it is taken by truck to a store, where you and other fans have the chance to purchase it.

KEY WORDS

- capital
- consumer
- demand
- entrepreneurship
- factor of production
- good
- labor
- market equilibrium
- need
- producer
- scarcity
- service
- shortage
- supply
- surplus
- want

Economic Basics

UNIT 4 / LESSON 1

Interpreting Sources: Supply and Demand Graph

Economists often show supply and demand using a graph. This kind of graph shows how much of any good or service producers are willing to supply at different prices, and how much consumers are willing to buy at different prices. If producers make more than consumers demand, they create a **surplus**. If they make too little, then there is a **shortage**. Ideally, producers and consumers will find the **market equilibrium**. This is the price at which producers make exactly as much as consumers want to buy.

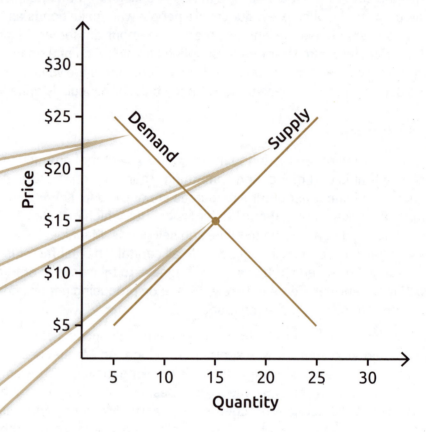

This part of the graph shows a shortage. Notice that demand is much higher than supply. Demand decreases as the price increases.

This part of the graph shows a surplus. Supply is much higher than demand. Producers are willing to make more of something when they can make big profits.

This point shows the market equilibrium. This is where the quantity producers are willing to supply and the quality consumers wish to purchase are equal.

Lesson Practice

UNIT 4 / LESSON 1

Complete the activities below to check your understanding of the lesson content.

KEY POINT!

Economics attempts to explain how people meet their wants and needs despite having a scarcity of resources.

Vocabulary

Match the term on the left with the correct definition on the right.

1. consumer

2. market equilibrium

3. need

4. producer

5. scarcity

6. supply

7. surplus

8. want

A. something people have to have to survive

B. the condition of not having enough of something for everyone to have what they want and need

C. too much of something; exceeds demand

D. person who buys a good or service

E. something people would like to have but do not have to have

F. how much of something producers make

G. person who makes and sells goods and services

H. the point at which supply and demand are equal

Lesson 1 / Economic Basics

UNIT 4 / LESSON 1

Lesson Practice

Apply Your Knowledge

Write one example of each type of factor of production on the lines below.

9. land
_____

10. labor
_____

11. capital
_____

12. entrepreneurship
_____

Skills Practice

Review the graph. Then choose the correct answer to each question.

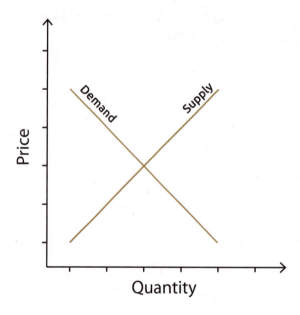

13. What conclusion about supply and demand does this graph best support?
    A People have unlimited wants.
    B Producers always make more and more of things.
    C Consumers always want to buy the most when prices are low.
    D Demand will eventually decline no matter what.

See page 171 for answers and help.

TEST STRATEGY

Read questions carefully to identify subject-specific terms and ideas. Question 13 includes many words related to economics, like *supply, demand, consumers,* and *producers.* Figure out the meanings of these words in order to answer the question correctly.

Economic Systems

UNIT 4 / LESSON 2

Organizing Economies

People must answer some basic economic questions in order to distribute goods and services: *What goods and services shall be produced? How shall goods and services be produced? For whom shall goods and services be produced?*

Different groups can decide the answers to these questions. The group that makes these decisions shapes the way economic systems work. Review the following table to learn about the four economic systems.

Type of Economic System	Who Answers Economic Questions
Command economy	Government leaders or planners answer all economic questions.
Market economy	Producers and consumers answer all economic questions.
Mixed economy	Government, producers, and consumers all have some say in answering the economic questions.
Traditional economy	People and groups answer the economic questions according to how they have done things over time.

What does this mean in practice? In the United States, producers and consumers make most decisions. Government also has a say, however. Companies must get licenses to broadcast over the radio, for example. In some cities, landlords can change rent by only so much each year. This creates a mixed economy.

KEY WORDS

- command economy
- market economy
- mixed economy
- traditional economy

UNIT 4 / LESSON 2

Lesson Practice

KEY POINT!

The four main economic systems are command, market, mixed, and traditional.

TEST STRATEGY

When you see questions that ask you to identify which option is not true, try using the process of elimination. Look at Question 2. First, make a mental list of who makes decisions in a market economy: producers and consumers. Then, eliminate anyone who could be in those groups. Is a business owner a producer? Is a central planner?

Complete the activities below to check your understanding of the lesson content.

Apply Your Knowledge

Read the text. Then choose the correct answer to each question.

1. Chinese economic planners carefully control the nation's economy. China is an example of a
   - A   command economy.
   - B   market economy.
   - C   mixed economy.
   - D   traditional economy.

2. Which of these groups does NOT make decisions in a market economy?
   - A   store owners
   - B   consumers
   - C   central planners
   - D   producers

3. How are mixed and market economies similar?
   - A   Both rely on producers to make all economic decisions.
   - B   Both have no government regulation.
   - C   Both usually have very rapid economic growth.
   - D   Both have a relatively free exchange of goods and services.

4. Country Y is home to a small population. People usually trade with each other for goods and services. They share important resources and do not use money. What generalization can you make about Country Y's economy?
   - A   It follows a traditional economic pattern.
   - B   It will not be able to sustain itself over time.
   - C   It probably will become a command economy.
   - D   It must have existed a long time ago.

See page 171 for answers and help.

Reading Charts, Graphs, and Tables

UNIT 4 / LESSON 3

Interpreting Charts and Graphs

The HiSET® will likely ask you to interpret some economic information given in a **chart** or **graph**. Charts and graphs are both visual representations of numerical information, or **data**. A chart often uses bars to show different levels across groups or over time. Pie charts are special charts that show parts of a whole using sections of a circle. A graph usually uses points on a line. People often use the words *charts* and *graphs* to mean the same thing, however.

Follow these steps to interpret charts and graphs:

Step 1: Read the title and labels on the horizontal and vertical axes.

Step 2: Figure out what each bar, line, or point represents. Review the legend or key if one is given.

Step 3: Determine the value of a bar or point by reading across from its highest level and down from its midpoint.

KEY WORDS

- chart
- data
- graph
- table

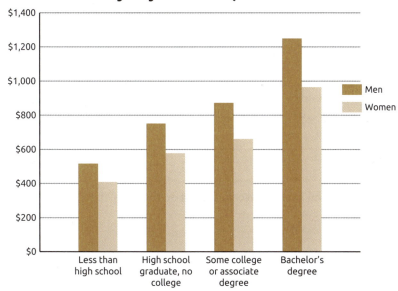

The vertical axis shows different dollar amounts. What does each of the bars represent?

Lesson 4 / Reading Charts, Graphs, and Tables

155

Reading Charts, Graphs, and Tables

Interpreting Tables

A **table** is another way to organize information. Tables have rows that run horizontally and columns that run vertically. Tables may give information and data using either words or numbers.

Follow these steps to interpret tables:

Step 1: Read the title of the table and any row or column headings.

Step 2: Determine what you need to find. Find specific information by placing your finger on the spot where the row and column data meet.

Step 3: Read horizontally or vertically to look for patterns and trends.

Review the following table. This table shows the same data as the previous bar graph. Think about what advantages and disadvantages the table has compared to the graph. The table makes it easier to see the exact figures shown, but it makes it a little harder to compare those figures across groups.

Median Weekly Pay by Education Level, 2014		
	Men	**Women**
Less than high school	$517	$409
High school graduate, no college	$751	$578
Some college or associate degree	$872	$661
Bachelor's degree	$1,249	$965

In this table, the columns are headed *Men* and *Women*. What do the rows show?

Lesson Practice

UNIT 4 / LESSON 3

Complete the activities below to check your understanding of the lesson content.

KEY POINT

Charts, graphs, and tables organize numerical information into a visual form. They allow viewers to interpret data to find patterns and draw conclusions.

Vocabulary

Write definitions in your own words for each of the key terms.

1. chart _____
   _____

2. data _____
   _____

3. graph _____
   _____

4. table _____
   _____

Apply Your Knowledge

Label the title, row headings, and column headings of the table below.

Average Price of Select Foods, 2014.		
	Eggs (per dozen)	Apples (per pound)
January	$2.00	$1.28
April	$2.12	$1.38
July	$1.95	$1.39
October	$1.95	$1.36

5. _____

6. _____

7. _____

Lesson 3 / Reading Charts, Graphs, and Tables

157

Lesson Practice

Skills Practice

Study the following graph. Then answer questions 8 and 9.

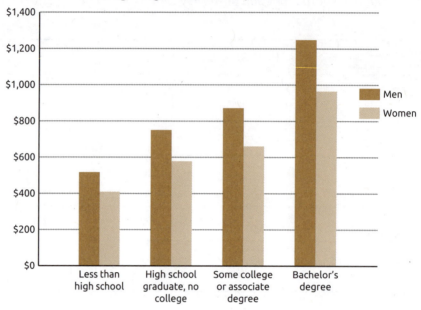

8. Which of these people likely makes about $775 per week?
   - A Mariel, a 19-year-old woman who dropped out of high school
   - B Devon, a 22-year-old man who passed his high school equivalency test
   - C Nikki, a 24-year-old woman who completed an associate's degree in nursing
   - D Stephan, a 26-year-old man who got a college degree in economics

9. Based on this graph, what conclusion about wages and education is best supported?
   - A People who complete more education earn higher wages than those with less education.
   - B The high costs of education are not justified by the wages people make.
   - C Graduating from high school is not worth the effort unless a person plans to attend college.
   - D Women benefit financially from attending college less than men do.

See page 171 for answers and help.

TEST STRATEGY

Read the question to figure out what it is really asking: *Which point on the graph is equal to about $775?* Put your finger at the right level on the vertical axis that shows dollars. Move it to the right until you find a bar that is about that height. What label does the horizontal axis have? Now, read the answer choices to find the one that best matches what you found.

Economic Indicators

UNIT 4 / LESSON 4

Patterns and Trends in the Economy

How do analysts measure the economy? One main way is by using **economic indicators**. Economic indicators are data that give suggestions about patterns in the economy. By studying this data, analysts can make predictions about the overall economy. They can consider whether it is likely to grow or shrink. They can also make generalizations, discussing how economic activity affects individuals and groups.

Some kinds of economic indicators give big-picture looks at the economy. The **gross domestic product (GDP)** of a nation is the value of all the goods and services it produced in a year. When the economy is growing, GDP goes up. When the economy shrinks, GDP goes down. Changes in economic growth and decline are normal. This process is called the **business cycle**.

The business cycle is closely related to another measurement, the **unemployment rate**. The unemployment rate tells the percentage of people who do not have jobs but are prepared to work. That means that this measurement includes people who are looking for work but excludes full-time students, for example. High unemployment shows problems in the overall economy. It is more likely to happen when the economy is shrinking.

Other economic indicators show how individuals are relating to the economy. The U.S. government creates a **consumer price index (CPI)**. This measurement shows how much it costs an average consumer to buy specific goods ranging from bread to clothing to medicines. Economists also measure **consumer confidence**. This measurement tells how people think the economy is doing. When consumer confidence is high, people feel good about their jobs and earnings. They are likely to buy more expensive goods like cars or televisions. The opposite is true when consumer confidence is low.

KEY WORDS

- business cycle
- consumer confidence
- consumer price index (CPI)
- economic indicator
- gross domestic product (GDP)
- unemployment rate

UNIT 4 / LESSON 4: Economic Indicators

Interpreting Sources: Homeownership Rate

U.S. economists look at figures like the homeownership rate to see how the economy is doing. Many Americans believe owning their own home is a sign of financial stability. People who own their own homes usually have more wealth than people who rent. This is because they gain control of the value of their property as their pay down their debt on it. Homes are also investments that may grow in value over time.

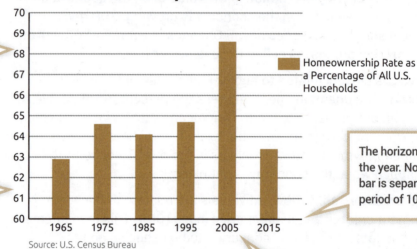

U.S. Homeownership Rates, 1965–2015

Source: U.S. Census Bureau

Look carefully at the range on each axis. A relatively small range like this one causes differences to appear greater than they really are on the graph.

The vertical axis shows the percentage of U.S. households who owned their own home.

The horizontal axis shows the year. Notice that each bar is separated by a period of 10 years.

All data shown reflects mid-year levels.

Notice that this bar is much higher than the others. A high-level economics question may ask you to consider reasons for this unusual difference. The homeownership rate was higher in the mid-2000s due to relaxed lending standards. Now notice that the bar is much lower in 2015. What might have happened during this time?

Lesson Practice

UNIT 4 / LESSON 4

Complete the activities below to check your understanding of the lesson content.

KEY POINT!

Economics attempts to explain how people meet their wants and needs despite having a scarcity of resources.

Vocabulary

Match the term on the left with the correct definition on the right.

1. business cycle

    A. measurement telling how people think the economy is doing

2. consumer confidence

    B. the value of all the goods and services a place produces in a year

3. consumer price index (CPI)

    C. percentage of people who do not have jobs but are looking for work

4. economic indicator

    D. measurement showing how much it costs an average consumer to buy specific goods

5. gross domestic product (GDP)

    E. growth and decline in the economy

6. unemployment rate

    F. statistic that gives suggestions about patterns in the economy

Lesson 4 / Economic Indicators

Lesson Practice

Skills Practice

Review the graph. Then choose the correct answer to each question.

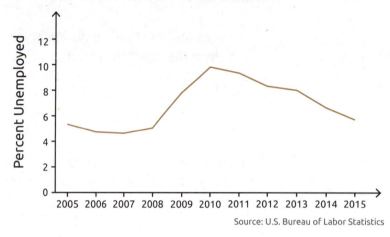

Unemployment Rate, 2005–2015

Source: U.S. Bureau of Labor Statistics

7. In which year was the unemployment rate the lowest?
   - A   2005
   - B   2007
   - C   2009
   - D   2014

8. Based on this graph, which statement about the U.S. economy is true?
   - A   Growth happened between 2014 and 2015 about as quickly as it did between 2007 and 2008.
   - B   The overall economy boomed in 2010 and 2011.
   - C   Problems led the economy to shrink between 2007 and 2010.
   - D   Economic growth was slow to restart after a sharp recession in 2006.

See page 171 for answers and help.

TEST STRATEGY

Focus on the most important ideas in each answer choice by underlining key words, phrases, and numbers. Read Question 8 and its answer choices. Circling words like *growth* and *boomed* will help you focus on the meanings of choices A and B.

Government and the Economy

UNIT 4 / LESSON 5

KEY WORDS

- labor movement
- labor union
- minimum wage
- regulation
- Wagner Act

Regulation and Legislation

Recall that in a pure market economy, government has no influence. All decisions are made by producers and consumers. During the 1800s, the United States came close to having a true market economy. The Constitution gave Congress the power to oversee commerce among the states and to set taxes on goods brought into and out of the country. But government leaders tried to avoid interfering in economic activity.

By the early 1900s, Americans wanted more government involvement in the economy. They pointed out that dishonest businesses sold unsafe goods or lied in their advertisements. They worried that business owners expected too much of their workers and paid them too little. A growing **labor movement** fought for the rights of workers. Employers, however, did not want their workers to join **labor unions**, organizations that tried to bargain on the behalf of all workers.

Government slowly began to increase its involvement in the economy. Laws like the Pure Food and Drug Act, passed in the early 1900s, placed new **regulations** on producers. Regulations are government rules. Other laws limited the hours women and young people were required to work, and barred young children from working at all. In the 1930s, the federal government passed the **Wagner Act**. This law guarantees workers the right to organize unions. It also sets up a federal agency to help manage disagreements between workers and employers.

Today, the government continues to exercise some say in economic activity. For example, the federal government sets a nationwide **minimum wage**. A minimum wage is the least amount of money per hour a worker must be paid. States and communities sometimes have their own higher minimum wages. Government policies also shape the activities of banks and financial institutions.

UNIT 4 / LESSON 5: Government and the Economy

Interpreting Sources: Equal Employment Opportunity Commission

The Civil Rights Act of 1964 used the power of the federal government against discrimination in many parts of U.S. society. One part of this law worked to limit workplace discrimination. The law created the Equal Employment Opportunity Commission (EEOC) to make sure the law was enforced fairly. The EEOC also manages disagreements related to the law.

Unlawful Employment Practices

(a) Employer Practices

It shall be an unlawful employment practice for an employer—

(1) to fail or refuse to hire or to discharge any individual, or otherwise to discriminate against any individual with respect to his compensation, terms, conditions, or privileges of employment, because of such individual's race, color, religion, sex, or national origin. . . .

> *This part of the law explains what employers may not legally do. They may not decline to hire someone or decide to fire someone just because of his or her race, religious beliefs, gender, or place of birth.*

(g) Powers of Commission

The Commission shall have power—

(1) to cooperate with and, with their consent, utilize regional, State, local, and other agencies, both public and private, and individuals. . . .

(3) to furnish to persons subject to this subchapter such technical assistance as they may request to further their compliance with this subchapter or an order issued thereunder;

(4) upon the request of (i) any employer, whose employees or some of them, or (ii) any labor organization, whose members or some of them, refuse or threaten to refuse to cooperate in effectuating the provisions of this subchapter, to assist in such effectuation by conciliation or such other remedial action as is provided by this subchapter. . . .

> *Laws and government documents often use complex words instead of more familiar words. Utilize means the same thing as use. Furnish means the same thing as give or provide. Use context clues to help figure out the meanings of unfamiliar words like these.*

> *This section has difficult language. But it simply says that the commission can help employers or organizations to make sure their employees abide by this law.*

Lesson Practice

UNIT 4 / LESSON 5

Complete the activities below to check your understanding of the lesson content.

Vocabulary

Complete each sentence with a key term from the lesson.

| labor union | minimum wage | regulation | Wagner Act |

1. The _____ guaranteed the right of workers to organize.

2. Laws set the lowest price for labor, also called the _____.

3. Government can issue a _____ to set rules for how businesses can behave.

4. Workers who join a _____ work together for better conditions and pay.

Skills Practice

Choose the correct answer to each question.

5. Which of these was NOT a problem in business by the early 1900s?
   - A Workers had few rights.
   - B Government supported a market economy.
   - C Businesses used false advertising.
   - D Children worked instead of going to school.

6. Labor unions supported laws limiting working hours. Which statement best explains this fact?
   - A Women and children were the main organizers of labor unions.
   - B People working many hours were less interested in being paid a minimum wage.
   - C Limiting hours meant businesses needed more workers to achieve the same results.
   - D Federal lawmakers who supported reducing working hours also supported organizing unions.

TEST STRATEGY

Remember to read questions carefully to see if they ask for something that is not true, like in Question 5. These questions can be especially tricky. Three of the answer choices will meet the conditions given in the question. One will not. Be sure to select the one that does not fit.

UNIT 4 / LESSON 5 — Lesson Practice

KEY POINT!

Government uses laws and regulations to help support economic growth and protect individual economic rights.

7. States and communities sometimes set their own minimum wage. Which reason best explains this practice?
   - A Citizens of some places have more education and job experience than those in other places.
   - B States legislatures have the right to overturn federal laws that do not meet their state's interests.
   - C Federal minimum wage laws do not apply to private business in states and communities.
   - D Some cities, like New York and Seattle, are more expensive to live in than the nation as a whole.

8. How did the Civil Rights Act of 1964 affect the economy?
   - A It placed new regulations on hiring practices.
   - B It protected the right of workers to organize.
   - C It limited what kind of speech could appear in advertisements.
   - D It helped minority entrepreneurs start new businesses.

See page 171 for answers and help.

Unit Test — UNIT 4

Answer the questions based on the content covered in this unit.

1. Which of these is NOT a factor of production?
   A entrepreneurship
   B labor
   C land
   D money

2. The market equilibrium is the point at which supply and demand are equal. What happens when a producer makes more of a good than is needed by the consumers?
   A There is a surplus.
   B There is a shortage.
   C Consumers increase demand.
   D Prices go up.

3. Which economic concept tells why people cannot have everything they want?
   A needs and wants
   B shortages
   C scarcity
   D opportunity cost

Read the following passage. Then, answer questions 4 and 5.

The Soviet Union was formed after a series of revolutions in 1917. At that time, Russia was fighting in World War I. Its people struggled to raise enough food to feed themselves and soldiers. Resources became scarce.

Revolutionaries who supported communist ideals overthrew the emperor. Soon, they took over the nation's factories and railroads. They decided to organize workers and resources in order to meet production goals. They claimed control of private lands and homes.

These actions set a precedent for the Soviet economy for decades to come. The nation used a communist system until its fall in the early 1990s.

4. Based on this passage, what kind of economic system did the Soviet Union have?
   A market
   B command
   C traditional
   D mixed

5. Consider this sentence from the passage.

   They decided to organize workers and resources in order to meet production goals.

   Which economic question does this sentence most answer?
   A What goods and services shall be produced?
   B How shall goods and services be produced?
   C When shall goods and services be produced?
   D For whom shall goods and services be produced?

UNIT 4 | Unit Test

Use the following text and table to answer questions 6–8.

The exchange rate is the price of one currency in terms of another. The rate of a currency to another is how much of the second currency the first one can buy.

Sample Exchange Rates, 2015		
Currency	U.S. $ to Currency	Currency to U.S. $
U.S. Dollar	1.00	1.00
Euro (European Union)	0.89	1.13
British Pound	0.65	1.54
Canadian Dollar	1.32	0.75
Japanese Yen	120.59	0.01

All rates are rounded.

6. According to the table, which of these currencies is the most valuable per unit?
   - A   Canadian Dollar
   - B   Japanese Yen
   - C   U.S. Dollar
   - D   British Pound

7. Based on this table, which two currencies have the value that is the most similar per unit?
   - A   Pound and Yen
   - B   U.S. Dollar and Euro
   - C   Canadian Dollar and U.S. Dollar
   - D   Pound and Euro

8. Margot is traveling from the United States to Paris, France. Which currency from the table should she purchase before leaving on her trip?
   - A   U.S. Dollar
   - B   Yen
   - C   Euro
   - D   Pound

Use the following graph to answer questions 9–11.

New Residential Housing Starts by Region, 2010 and 2014

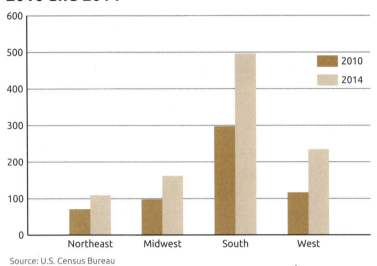

Source: U.S. Census Bureau

All numbers are given in thousands.

9. Based on this graph, which U.S. region is likely experiencing the most population growth?
    A   Northeast
    B   Midwest
    C   South
    D   West

10. By about how much did housing starts grow in the Northeast between 2010 and 2014?
    A   by about 10,000
    B   by about 35,000
    C   by about 100,000
    D   by about 200,000

11. What conclusion about the U.S. economy is best supported by this graph?
    A   Housing prices became unaffordable between 2010 and 2014.
    B   Government regulation of housing decreased between 2010 and 2014.
    C   More people had to leave their homes in 2014 than in 2010.
    D   Economic conditions improved significantly between 2010 and 2014.

UNIT 4 — Unit Test

Read the excerpts from the following speeches. Then, answer questions 12–14.

From a speech by President Barack Obama:

So the actions that have been taken in just four states—Maryland, Connecticut, Minnesota, and Hawaii—means that over a million workers will see a raise. What's more, we've seen big companies like The Gap, and small businesses—from a pizza joint in St. Louis to an ice cream parlor in Florida—increasingly choosing to raise wages for their employees because they know it's good business. They know that it means employees are more likely to stay on the job, less turnover. It means that they're going to be more productive, and customers see the difference.

From a speech by Senator Ted Cruz:

Far better than the promise of $10.10 an hour, is $46.98—the wage Americans can earn in the oil and gas industry. We ought to come together with bipartisan unanimity to say we will stand with the American people to bring millions of jobs, raise median income, and make it easier for people who are struggling to achieve the American Dream. We should all come together and vote on the American Energy Renaissance Act, to remove government barriers and open up new federal lands and resources to develop high-paying, promising jobs that expand opportunity.

12. Based on these excerpts, which inference about the minimum wage is best supported?
    A Workers who earn the minimum wage struggle to get ahead.
    B The minimum wage is set by businesses and industries.
    C Relatively few retail and restaurant workers earn the minimum wage.
    D Increasing the level of the minimum wage will hurt the energy industry.

13. Which statement best summarizes President Obama's point of view on the minimum wage?
    A It should be abolished to help businesses grow quickly.
    B It should be higher at large companies than at small ones.
    C It should be raised in order to help workers and businesses.
    D It should be grown to about 45 dollars per hour to be competitive.

14. Which solution does Senator Cruz propose to deal with low wages?
    A helping higher-paying industries grow
    B raising the minimum wage so workers earn more
    C training workers for jobs on federal lands and preserves
    D passing laws to encourage workers to stay in the same job

See page 171 for answers and help.

Unit Answer Key — UNIT 4

Lesson 1
1. D.
2. H.
3. A.
4. G. You can quickly categorize the terms on the left by category to help identify answers. For example, *consumer* and *producer* are the only two terms for types of people. This will help you easily identify the two possible answers: D. and G. both begin with person.
5. B.
6. F.
7. C.
8. E.
9. Sample answer: Wheat grows on land.
10. Sample answer: A baker makes wheat bread.
11. Sample answer: A baker uses an oven to make bread.
12. Sample answer: A person decides to open a store to sell the bread.
13. C. See the Test Strategy for more help on this item.

Lesson 2
1. A. China's economy is controlled by the government.
2. C. See the Test Strategy for more help on this item.
3. D. Producers and consumers both have input.
4. A. The people have developed a system over time that works for them.

Lesson 3
1. a visual representation of data; also called a graph
2. information given as numbers
3. a visual representation of data; also called a chart
4. a visual representation of information using words or numbers
5. title
6. column heading
7. row heading
8. B. See the Test Strategy for more help on this item.
9. A.

Lesson 4
1. E.
2. A.
3. D.
4. F.
5. B.
6. C.
7. B. Look for the lowest point on the line, and then look at the date.
8. C. See the Test Strategy for more help on this item.

Lesson 5
1. Wagner Act
2. minimum wage
3. regulation
4. labor union
5. B. See the Test Strategy for more help on this item.
6. C. Labor unions protect the rights and jobs of workers.
7. D. Cost of living varies from place to place, so it would be unfair not to adjust the minimum wage accordingly.
8. A. The law makes it illegal for employers to discriminate against applicants or workers.

Unit Test
1. D.
2. A.
3. C.
4. B.
5. B.
6. D.
7. B.
8. C.
9. C.
10. B.
11. D.
12. A.
13. C.
14. A.

Unit Glossary

- **business cycle** — growth and decline in the economy over time
- **capital** — goods used to make other goods
- **chart** — a visual representation of data; also called a graph
- **command economy** — economic system in which government or central planners make all economic decisions
- **consumer** — person who buys a good or service
- **consumer confidence** — measurement telling how people think the economy is doing
- **consumer price index (CPI)** — measurement showing how much it costs an average consumer to buy specific goods
- **data** — information given as numbers
- **demand** — how much of something consumers demand
- **economic indicator** — piece of data that gives suggestions about patterns in the economy
- **entrepreneurship** — the willingness to take risks to start a business
- **factor of production** — resource used to make goods and services
- **good** — physical object made for consumption
- **graph** — a visual representation of data; also called a chart
- **gross domestic product (GDP)** — the value of all the goods and services a place produces in a year
- **labor** — the efforts of workers
- **labor movement** — movement to fight for the rights of workers
- **labor union** — organization that tried to bargain on the behalf of workers
- **market economy** — economic system in which producers and consumers make all economic decisions
- **market equilibrium** — the point at which supply and demand are equal
- **minimum wage** — lowest amount a person can be paid per hour
- **mixed economy** — economic system in which producers, consumers, and government all make economic decisions
- **need** — something people have to have to survive
- **producer** — person who makes and sells goods and services
- **regulation** — a rule set by the government
- **scarcity** — the condition of not having enough of something for everyone to have what they want and need
- **service** — something done for someone else
- **shortage** — having too little of something to meet demand
- **supply** — how much of something producers make
- **surplus** — having too much of something to meet demand
- **table** — a visual representation of information using words or numbers set in rows and columns
- **traditional economy** — economic system in which people make decisions based on how things have been done over time
- **unemployment rate** — percentage of people who do not have jobs but are looking for work
- **Wagner Act** — law that guarantees workers the right to organize
- **want** — something people would like to have but do not have to have

Study More! — UNIT 4

Economic Basics
- Prices
- Opportunity cost
- Trade-offs
- Microeconomics and macroeconomics

Economic Systems
- Role of government in mixed economies
- Communism
- Socialism

Reading Charts, Graphs, and Tables
- Pie charts
- Line graphs
- Gathering statistics and data

Economic Indicators
- Other economic indicators, such as the inflation rate and money supply
- Economic forecasting

Government and the Economy
- Rent control laws
- Federal Reserve System
- Income taxes
- Deficit spending and the national debt

PRACTICE TEST | Social Studies

Answer the following questions based on the material you have learned.

Questions 1–3 refer to the following map.

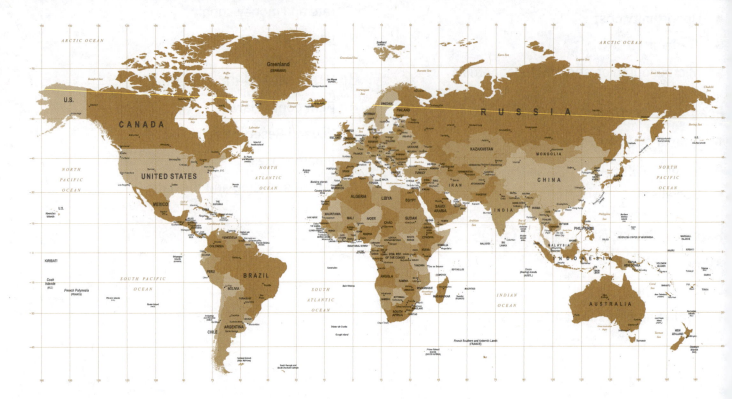

1. Which of the following correctly describes the map shown here?
    A   It is a climate map.
    B   It is a political map.
    C   It is a thematic map.
    D   It is an economic map.

2. This map would be MOST useful for determining
    A   distances between nations.
    B   average annual rainfall in a specific country.
    C   geological features of a particular continent.
    D   differences in population density throughout various regions.

3. Which term would be the MOST helpful in explaining why Greenland appears similar in size to South America on this map?
    A   key
    B   Bantu
    C   Mercator
    D   projection

PRACTICE TEST

4. Which term names a ruling family of ancient China, India, or Sumer?
   A   caravel
   B   republic
   C   democracy
   D   dynasty

5. Which of the following has the MOST direct governmental authority in a republic?
   A   adult citizens
   B   elected representatives
   C   military leaders
   D   religious leaders

6. Which of the following is a state-level position similar to that of president?
   A   governor
   B   mayor
   C   city manager
   D   attorney general

7. Which of the following classic civilizations was known as the central Greek military power?
   A   Athens
   B   Rome
   C   Sparta
   D   Alexandria

Questions 8–11 refer to the following chart.

Types of Economies
1. Economic activity is under government control.
2. Economic activity is determined by the actions of producers and consumers.
3. Economic activity is determined by producers, consumers, and the government.
4. Economic activity is determined by custom and habit.

8. What type of economy is described on line 1?
   A   a command economy
   B   a mixed economy
   C   a traditional economy
   D   a market economy

9. What type of economy is described on line 2?
   A   a mixed economy
   B   a traditional economy
   C   a market economy
   D   a command economy

10. What type of economy is described on line 3?
    A   a traditional economy
    B   a mixed economy
    C   a command economy
    D   a market economy

11. What type of economy is described on line 4?
    A   a market economy
    B   a command economy
    C   a traditional economy
    D   a mixed economy

PRACTICE TEST

12. Which statement BEST explains how voting laws are set forth and modified?
    A They are set forth and modified for all elections by individual state governments.
    B They are set forth and modified for all elections by Congress.
    C They are set forth in the Constitution and modified when necessary by Congress.
    D They are set forth and modified by state governments for state elections and by Congress for federal elections.

Questions 13 and 14 refer to the following figure.

13. Which of the following BEST replaces the center section of this timeline?
    A Dark Ages
    B Reformation
    C Byzantine Empire
    D the Hundred Years' War

14. Which statement about that period is the MOST accurate?
    A It is considered a time of cultural rebirth.
    B It witnessed the onset of international trade.
    C Little is known of its history.
    D Several new sects of Christianity formed during this time.

Questions 15–17 refer to the following passage.

Article III. Section 1.

The _____ Power of the United States, shall be vested in one supreme Court, and in such inferior Courts as the Congress may from time to time ordain and establish. The Judges, both of the supreme and inferior Courts, shall hold their Offices during good Behaviour, and shall, at stated Times, receive for their Services, a Compensation, which shall not be diminished during their Continuance in Office.

— The United States Constitution

15. Which word belongs in the blank in the passage shown?
    A federal
    B legislative
    C executive
    D judicial

16. Which other part of government is given some authority over that branch in this passage?
    A the federal branch
    B the legislative branch
    C the executive branch
    D the judicial branch

17. Which of the following BEST describes that relationship?
    A It is a charter.
    B It is an example of lobbying.
    C It is an example of checks and balances.
    D It is a bicameral legislature.

18. What was Christopher Columbus's destination when he set sail on behalf of Spain?
   A the coast of Africa
   B East Asia
   C the West Indies
   D South America

19. During the era of European colonization, enslaved Africans were shipped to the Americas as part of a globalized economic system involving
   A two basic trade routes.
   B three basic trade routes.
   C four basic trade routes.
   D five basic trade routes.

Questions 20 and 21 refer to the following image.

20. The written text shown here would be MOST useful to a historian as
   A a primary source of information on ancient hunter-gatherer groups.
   B a secondary source of information on life during the Renaissance.
   C a primary source of information on ancient Egyptian culture.
   D a secondary source of information on Athenian democracy.

21. This image displays an early example of human
   A agriculture.
   B technology.
   C urbanization.
   D industrialization.

22. Which of the following is an example of a Mesoamerican civilization?
   A the Aztec
   B the Mississippians
   C the Andes
   D the Spartans

PRACTICE TEST

Questions 23 and 24 refer to the following passage.

1. Resolved, That California, with suitable boundaries, ought, upon her application to be admitted as one of the States of this Union, without the imposition by Congress of any restriction in respect to the exclusion or introduction of slavery within those boundaries.

— Compromise of 1850

23. Which of the following was enacted as part of the legislation quoted in the passage?
    A the Fugitive Slave Act
    B the Wagner Act
    C the Homestead Act
    D the Kansas-Nebraska Act

24. Which of these ideas is MOST related to the spirit of this legislation?
    A Manifest Destiny
    B nationalism
    C self-government
    D popular sovereignty

Question 25 refers to the following image.

25. Which of the following specifically protects the right being exercised here?
    A the Kansas-Nebraska Act
    B the Civil Rights Act of 1964
    C the Pure Food and Drug Act
    D the Wagner Act of 1935

26. Which of the following is MOST closely associated with the Progressive Era?
    A feminism
    B the Great Depression
    C muckraking
    D the New Deal

27. To which of these nations did the United States send troops when it launched its War on Terror?
    A the Soviet Union
    B China
    C Germany
    D Afghanistan

28. Who among the following do historians believe contributed to the Federalist Papers?
    A Thomas Jefferson
    B George Washington
    C Preston Brooks
    D Alexander Hamilton

29. Who among the following participates in Congress ONLY to cast a tie-breaking vote?
    A the president
    B the vice president
    C the Speaker of the House
    D the Electoral College

Questions 30–32 refer to the following figure.

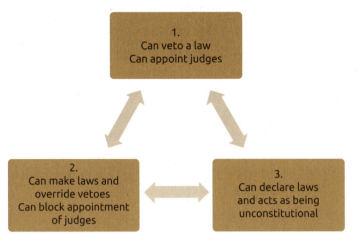

30. Who among the following is described in box 1?
    A the President
    B the Chief Justice of the Supreme Court
    C the Speaker of the House
    D the United States Attorney General

31. Who among the following belongs in box 2?
    A the President
    B a Senator
    C an Associate Supreme Court Justice
    D the Secretary of State

32. Who among the following belongs in box 3?
    A a Senator
    B the Secretary of Homeland Security
    C a State Representative
    D the Chief Justice of the Supreme Court

33. Which of the following does NOT exist when a market is in a state of equilibrium?
    A scarcity
    B capital
    C surplus
    D demand

Question 34 and 35 refer to the following graph.

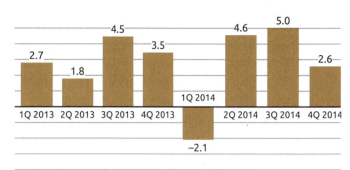

Source: CNN

34. This graph MOST directly gives information on
    A an important economic indicator.
    B changes in market equilibrium.
    C growth and decline in supply.
    D changes in the unemployment rate.

35. According to the graph, which period witnessed the steepest economic decline?
    A the first half of 2013
    B the fourth quarter of 2013
    C the first quarter of 2014
    D the second half of 2014

36. Which of the following MOST directly threatened a Constitutional check on presidential power?
    A President George Washington's establishment of the first White House Cabinet
    B President George W. Bush's deployment of troops to Afghanistan
    C President Franklin D. Roosevelt's court-packing plan
    D President Andrew Jackson's opposition to the Bank of the United States

Questions 37 and 38 refer to the following passage.

Legislation is powerless to eradicate racial instincts or to abolish distinctions based upon physical differences, and the attempt to do so can only result in accentuating the difficulties of the present situation. If the civil and political rights of both races be equal, one cannot be inferior to the other civilly or politically. If one race be inferior to the other socially, the Constitution of the United States cannot put them upon the same plane.

— *Plessy* v. *Ferguson* (1896)

37. Which of the following legal principles does the Supreme Court uphold in this decision?
    A judicial review
    B executive privilege
    C separate but equal
    D judicial activism

38. Which of the following Supreme Court decisions reversed this one?
    A *McCulloch* v. *Maryland*
    B *Brown* v. *Board of Education of Topeka, Kansas*
    C *Dred Scott* v. *Sandford*
    D *Miranda* v. *Arizona*

39. Which of the following do historians consider the earliest example of American self-government?
    A Jamestown, Virginia
    B the Southern Colonies
    C Plymouth Colony
    D New Amsterdam

40. Weaknesses in which of the following led to the drafting and ratification of the U.S. Constitution?
    A the Declaration of Independence
    B the Proclamation of 1763
    C the Second Continental Congress
    D the Articles of Confederation

41. Which of the following statements is an example of an opinion?
    A Political parties existed before the Civil War.
    B George Washington opposed political parties.
    C Political parties are a threat to liberty.
    D Primary elections are a method by which political parties choose candidates.

42. Which of the following was founded primarily to oppose slavery?
    A the Republican Party
    B the Democratic Party
    C the Electoral College
    D the Continental Congress

43. A citizen who works to influence laws and policies on behalf of a private group is called a _____.
    A governor
    B candidate
    C lobbyist
    D caravel

44. Which of the following is an argument made by opponents of the DREAM Act?
    A Those who enter the country illegally should not be allowed to become citizens.
    B Local authorities are best able to oversee and administer city services.
    C A person under the age of 18 is not mature enough to vote responsibly.
    D *Marbury* v. *Madison* established the power of judicial review.

Question 45 refers to the following chart.

Labor
Capital
Entrepreneurship
Natural Resources

45. Which of the following is the BEST title for this chart?
    A Types of Scarcity
    B Goods and Services
    C Factors of Production
    D Important Economic Terms

46. Which of the following is an example of a functional document?
    A a property deed
    B a tax form
    C a city map
    D a charter

47. A Cabinet is a feature of which part of the government?
    A the Supreme Court
    B the Senate
    C the executive branch
    D the House of Representatives

48. Which of the following did the U.S. Constitution establish that the Articles of Confederation had not?
    A a legislative branch
    B an amendment process
    C a procedure for collecting taxes
    D an executive leader

49. Which of the following MOST contributed to the creation of the first permanent human settlements?
    A farming
    B gathering
    C writing
    D hunting

50. Which of the following statements is an example of a fact?
    A Living in Antarctica would be very unpleasant.
    B Antarctica is the southernmost continent.
    C Antarctica is the most densely populated continent.
    D People will never have a good reason to explore Antarctica.

Practice Test Answer Key

1. B.	18. B.	35. C.
2. A.	19. B.	36. C.
3. C.	20. C.	37. C.
4. D.	21. B.	38. B.
5. B.	22. A.	39. C.
6. A.	23. A.	40. D.
7. C.	24. D.	41. C.
8. A.	25. D.	42. A.
9. C.	26. C.	43. C.
10. B.	27. D.	44. A.
11. C.	28. D.	45. C.
12. A.	29. B.	46. B.
13. A.	30. A.	47. C.
14. C.	31. B.	48. D.
15. D.	32. D.	49. A.
16. B.	33. C.	50. B.
17. C.	34. A.	

NOTES

NOTES

NOTES

NOTES

NOTES

NOTES

NOTES

NOTES

NOTES

NOTES